THE NOTARY'S GUIDE TO LOUISIANA CEMETERY LAW

THE NOTARY'S GUIDE TO LOUISIANA CEMETERY LAW

Authority, Documentation, and Practice Under Title 8

A comprehensive guide for Notaries Public
on Louisiana Cemetery Law

JOSHUA R. LEBLANC

Bayou State
PUBLISHING

For permission requests, contact:
Bayou State Publishing
P.O. Box 1049
Abbeville, LA 70511
Email: info@bayoustatepublishing.com
Website: bayoustatepublishing.com

ISBN: 978-1-970659-05-4

Printed in the United States of America
First Edition, 2026

Published by **Bayou State Publishing**
Youngsville, LA

Disclaimer:
The information contained in this book is provided for general educational and informational purposes only. Nothing in this book should be construed as, or relied upon as, legal advice. Laws and regulations vary by jurisdiction and are subject to change. Readers are strongly encouraged to consult with a qualified attorney before making any decisions or taking any action based on the material presented herein. The author and publisher expressly disclaim any liability for actions taken or not taken based on the contents of this book.

ABOUT THE AUTHOR

Joshua R. LeBlanc serves as the Executive Director of Holy Family Cemetery in New Iberia, Louisiana. He was ordained a Catholic deacon for the Diocese of Lafayette in 2016 and is currently assigned to St. Martin de Tours Catholic Church in St. Martinville.

Deacon LeBlanc brings a unique combination of theological insight, pastoral care, and administrative precision to the sacred work of cemetery management.

He holds a Master of Arts in Moral Theology and a +30 in Bioethics from Holy Apostles College and Seminary and is certified in Bioethics by the National Catholic Bioethics Center. He is currently pursuing a Doctorate in the field of Bioethics.

In addition to his ministry and administrative leadership, Deacon LeBlanc is a commissioned Civil Law Notary Public in and for the State of Louisiana and the owner of two small businesses – an IT firm and Chesterton's Fine Cigars in Youngsville, La. It is through this background that he shares his expertise in faith, ethics, and cemetery law.

Deacon LeBlanc also serves as a police chaplain and reserve police officer for the Youngsville and Abbeville Police Departments. He is also chaplain for the Military and Hospitaller Order of St. Lazarus of Jerusalem in the rank of Ecclesiastical Commander, whose mission is to serve the sick and dying. He is the Delegate for the Imperial Calcasieu Delegation and Vice Chancellor for Communications for the Grand Priory of America

As a deacon, he has ministered to grieving families for years, guiding them through the Catholic Church's teachings on death, burial, and resurrection. As a professional cemetery administrator, he has developed robust compliance systems rooted in Louisiana law, ensuring that every interment, fund, and record upholds both the dignity of the deceased and the legal obligations of the living.

Deacon LeBlanc is the author of *The Louisiana Cemetery Form Book: Legal Documents, Templates, and Compliance Tools for Cemetery Authorities and Notaries Public*, the companion book in this series. Together, these works form the foundation of *The Louisiana Cemetery Authority Series,* a comprehensive legal and operational reference for religious and civil cemetery professionals throughout the state.

He and his wife, Annie, reside in Abbeville, Louisiana, with their cat Benedict.

THE LOUISIANA CEMETERY AUTHORITY SERIES

The Louisiana Cemetery Handbook: Law, Compliance, and Administration: A comprehensive guide to Louisiana cemetery law, Title 8 statutes, case law, and regulatory compliance.

The Louisiana Cemetery Forms Book: Documents, Templates, and Compliance Tools for Cemetery Authorities and Notaries Public. A companion volume containing practical forms, sample contracts, affidavits, and checklists for daily operations.

Catholic and Cultural Burial Traditions in Louisiana: A Guide to Faith, Heritage, and Sacred Practice. A comprehensive exploration of Louisiana's Catholic, Cajun, Creole, African American, and Native burial customs, offering theological insight, cultural history, and practical guidance for cemetery professionals and families.

Louisiana Cemetery Case Law: Jurisprudence, Practical Lessons, and Title 8 in the Courts. A clear and practical guide to Louisiana's major cemetery cases, this volume explains how courts interpret Title 8 in real-world disputes involving burial authority, disinterment, family cemeteries, undeveloped land sales, trust funds, and historic burial protections.

The Notary's Guide to Louisiana Cemetery Law: Authority, Documentation, and Practice Under Title 8. A practical reference that equips Louisiana notaries with clear, compliant language, clauses, and pastoral guidance for navigating cemetery ownership, interment rights, and Title 8 obligations in everyday notarial practice.

THE LOUISIANA CEMETERY HANDBOOK

Law, Compliance, and Administration

The ***Louisiana Cemetery Handbook*** is the state's most comprehensive and authoritative guide to the legal, historical, and operational foundations of cemetery management in Louisiana. Written for cemetery authorities, notaries public, attorneys, clergy, and municipal officials, it explains—in clear and practical language—**how Louisiana's unique burial laws work** and how they should be applied in everyday cemetery operations.

This essential volume includes:

- **A full explanation of Louisiana's cemetery laws**, including Title 8, Louisiana Civil Code, and relevant Administrative Code provisions.
- **Historical and cultural background** that illuminates why Louisiana's cemetery laws are distinct from those of any other state.
- **Detailed commentary on interment rights, perpetual care, abandonment procedures, dedication and removal, disinterment, merchandise trust laws, succession issues, and more.**
- **Best-practice guidelines** for cemetery operations, recordkeeping, trust fund compliance, and consumer protection.
- **Practical examples, case studies, and diagrams** to help cemetery personnel apply the law correctly.
- **Professional insights** informed by the author's experience in cemetery administration, notarial practice, and pastoral ministry.

TABLE OF CONTENTS

Introduction 2

Chapter 1
Why Cemetery Law Matters to Notaries 9

Chapter 2
Overview of Louisiana Cemetery Law 23

Chapter 3
Understanding Cemetery Property 35

Chapter 4
Who Has Authority? 49

Chapter 5
Authentic Acts Related to Cemetery Rights 59

Chapter 6
Transfers, Assignments, & Mutual Waiver Agreements 73

Chapter 7
Affidavit of Heirship of Burial Rights 85

Chapter 8
Consignment Agreement and Acknowledgment 95

Chapter 9
Acknowledgement of Right of Interment 105

Chapter 10
Disinterment and Reinterment Authorization.................................115

Chapter 11
Indigent and Communal Burial Programs 125

Chapter 12
Case Scenarios for Notarial Practice...133

Chapter 13
When You Must Say No 145

Chapter 14
Working with Cemeteries, Funeral Homes, and Courts 153

Conclusion 173

Glossary of Key Terms..179

General Index 185

INTRODUCTION

Cemetery matters place the Louisiana notary in a unique position – one that combines long-term documentation, family stewardship, and careful adherence to statutory requirements. A burial space may be used only once, but the instruments that govern its use often circulate for decades. When a transfer, waiver of rights, declarations of burial designations, or acknowledgment is needed, the notary's work may be the only surviving written link between past decisions and present needs. Unlike typical transactional practice, where documents often lose their relevance once filed or fulfilled, cemetery documentation remains active across generations, returning at moments when clarity is most needed and most emotionally charged.

Louisiana's cemetery law framework is rooted primarily in **Title 8 of the Louisiana Revised Statutes**, which establishes rules unlike those found in traditional property law. Cemetery spaces are not conveyed as land; they confer **a servitude of use - rights of interment**. The distinction is foundational. It shapes how authority is documented, how families make decisions, and how notaries prepare instruments that must align with statutory expectations, operational requirements, and future continuity of use. While notaries may work with acts that resemble conveyances, these instruments govern **human remains, successor authority, and vested burial rights** – a distinctly different legal terrain.

THE NOTARY'S RESPONSIBILITY IN CEMETERY MATTERS

Although the notary's authority is significant, it is also specific. A notary may:

- authenticate signatures,
- draft conveyances, such as sales agreements and Acts of Donation between private parties
- prepare instruments that reflect agreed-upon authority,
- document lineage and successor status,
- and confirm identity and consent.

But a notary may **not:**

- decide who has authority,
- interpret statutory priority,
- adjudicate conflicts among successors,
- or override cemetery operational requirements.

The role is defined by **neutral documentation**, not legal interpretation. This distinction is essential because families frequently approach notaries with unresolved disagreements, unclear expectations, or assumptions derived from property ownership, inheritance, or personal history. In those moments, restraint is not disengagement – it is professionalism. The notary's responsibility is to **wait for clarity before drafting**, not attempt to create clarity by drafting prematurely.

In cemetery matters, **neutrality is a discipline.** The notary must maintain it consistently, especially when one party pressures for action that another opposes, or when the cemetery's operational acceptance may be uncertain. The most effective cemetery notaries are those who:

prepare instruments only when authority is established,

- prepare instruments with precise legal language,
- confirm spousal status even when everyone assumes it is irrelevant,
- and preserve documentation in a form that future decision-makers can rely on with confidence.

AUTHORITY, CONSENT, AND THE TIME HORIZON OF CEMETERY WORK

Authority in cemetery matters is often misunderstood. Individuals are accustomed to thinking in terms of ownership, succession, or control of land. Cemetery rights do not align cleanly with those categories. The **right of interment** is not identical to ownership of real property but is rather an encumbrance of the cemetery's property — s**pousal burial rights under La. R.S. 8:805** persists until waived, regardless of whether successors believe those rights are still meaningful. These distinctions matter because instruments that ignore them may function today but fail decades later when a cemetery requires clarification.

Similarly, **consent** is a concept that varies depending on the proposed action.

For example:

- **Disposition of remains and/or disinterment** may be authorized by a **majority of adult children** under **La. R.S. 8:655** if no spouse survives and if no **Notarial Declaration or Testament** exists to the contrary.
- **Transfer of burial rights** may require a spousal waiver depending on how rights have vested.

A notary who treats all signatures as equivalent, or all actions as requiring the same signatures, risks drafting instruments that are incomplete, unenforceable, or unacceptable to the cemetery.

Yet, once those requirements are met, the notary's work becomes enduring. In few areas does documentation maintain such longevity.

Instruments drafted today may be examined:

- when a spouse dies twenty years later,
- when grandchildren seek disinterment thirty years later,
- or when cemeteries change administration and request documentation from the prior generation to authorize a transfer or use of space.

Notarial documentation in cemetery matters is not just paperwork – it is part of the **continuity of memory and authority**. Even minor errors can echo long after the original signatories have passed away.

WHY CEMETERY LAW REQUIRES PRECISION

Cemetery law intersects with property law, succession law, and statutory regulation, but does not mirror any of them exactly. Rights of interment are typically created by purchase and recorded through cemetery administration, yet the **legal structure of Title 8** imposes obligations and restrictions that outlive the purchaser. Spousal burial rights may attach to a space, and notaries must be aware of that fact. Successor authority may arise through lineage rather than recordation. In some cases, clarity requires both: **documented lineage and operational acceptance.** Cemetery Authorities should be aware of the legal requirements in their cemeteries, but unfortunately, that is not always the case. Today's notary must be vigilant and know the requirements of Louisiana law so they may properly draft instruments that will most probably outlive them.

This framework means the Louisiana notary must avoid assumptions that arise naturally from other settings:

- **"If I paid for it, so I can transfer it."**
  Not necessarily.
- **"We don't need dad's spouse to agree."**
  Spousal rights persist until waived or transferred.
- **"You notarized it, so the cemetery has to accept it."**
  Operational acceptance and notarial validity are separate.
- **"An affidavit of heirship makes me the sole authority."**
  It documents lineage – but authority may still be shared.

Instruments must be crafted with precision because they are:

- used at moments of grief,
- reviewed by administrators unfamiliar with the original parties,
- and relied upon decades after execution.

The future reader of the document may not know the notary, the family, or the context. The instrument must therefore **speak clearly on its own.**

Neutrality, Refusal, and the Protection of the Public

Cemetery documentation often arises from difficult circumstances: deaths without instructions, estranged families, succession disputes, or decades-old assumptions. Notaries encounter requests that may seem reasonable but exceed their authority:

- *"Just notarize that I'm the one in charge."*
- *"Draft it so my brother can't interfere later."*
- *"We don't need to tell the cemetery that she disagrees."*
- *"You can just fix this old document, right?"*
- *"If you sign it, they'll accept it."*

In such moments, the notary protects the public not by drafting but by declining to draft.

A refusal is not adversarial; it maintains the boundary that ensures all subsequent actions rest on lawful, neutral, and operationally reliable documentation. The decision to say **no** is often the most responsible act a cemetery notary can take.

Acceptance, Authority, and the Operator's Discretion

Even perfectly drafted instruments do not override cemetery policies and rules. Cemeteries — whether municipal, religious, or private — retain **complete operational discretion** in determining what documentation is required before interment, disinterment, memorialization, or transfer. Operational acceptance does not rewrite the law; instead, it determines whether an action may occur within the cemetery. For this reason, **coordination precedes drafting.** The notary should understand a cemetery's expectations before preparing the instrument that must meet them. Before preparing any documents for a family, ALWAYS contact the cemetery to determine their requirements, especially regarding forms.

A document may be valid under Title 8 but still be rejected by the Cemetery if procedural requirements are not met.

The notary's goal is not merely validity – it is **reliability in use**.

What This Book Provides – and What It Does Not

This book offers:

- terminology that prevents ambiguity,
- distinctions that clarify authority,
- principles for determining when drafting begins,
- and guidance on when to stop drafting.

It does **not**:

- interpret disputes,
- advise on litigation strategy,
- override cemetery requirements,
- or provide legal conclusions regarding contested authority.

The intent of this book is simple:

to support Louisiana notaries in cemetery practice by reinforcing clarity, precision, neutrality, and continuity.

A Final Reflection Before Beginning

Cemetery work is not merely procedural. It touches the places where families return to grieve, remember, and connect with their past. The instruments a notary prepares may allow a family to bury a loved one without conflict. They may allow remains to be reinterred years later. They may prevent a dispute that otherwise would erupt at a moment of loss. And they may do so long after every person who signed them is gone.

The Louisiana notary occupies a quiet but essential role in this work. By clearly documenting authority, conscientiously confirming consent, responsibly protecting spousal rights, and consistently maintaining neutrality, the notary ensures that the future can act with confidence **rather than confusion.**

That is the purpose and discipline of cemetery notarial practice – and the purpose of this book.

This guidebook was published in January 2026

All citations from the Louisiana Revised Statutes 8 are from the 2024 edition unless otherwise noted.

CHAPTER 1

WHY CEMETERY LAW MATTERS TO NOTARIES

Cemetery issues arise in notarial practice more often than most new notaries expect. In Louisiana, the disposition of remains, the rights associated with burial spaces, and the authority to authorize transfers or disinterments fall at the intersection of **property law, succession law, and Title 8 of the Louisiana Revised Statutes**.

Families frequently approach notaries for guidance because many cemetery-related transactions require a written instrument, acknowledgment, Authentic Act, or affidavit to validate a transfer or confirm a chain of authority. Often, Cemetery Authorities are unaware of the legal requirements themselves, so they send families wishing to transfer cemetery spaces directly to Notaries. The notary does not perform cemetery operations, but the notary frequently **documents** the legal authority **that permits those operations**. This distinction is critical and defines the scope of notarial involvement.

Notaries do not grant burial rights — they record, confirm, or transfer rights established by law, contract, title instruments, or succession.

In many cases, notarial transactions concerning cemeteries do not take effect immediately. The Cemetery office functions in a manner similar to a clerk of court, and most transactions do not take legal effect until they are received, accepted, and recorded by the Cemetery

Authority. This is even true for Acts of Donation in addition to sales of burial rights.

§8:802(A) - Transfer of ownership rights
In order to insure that at all times the cemetery authority will have complete and accurate records, the sale or transfer of any right of interment or cemetery space, shall not be binding upon a cemetery authority until approved in writing by a duly authorized officer, agent or employee of the cemetery authority and duly recorded in the official records of the cemetery.

As a result, the notary's role is often the first step in resolving questions of who may be buried, who controls a space, and who may authorize disinterment or reinterment. Clarity in documentation prevents conflict, delays, and litigation — and ensures families and cemetery authorities can act confidently during periods of emotional stress.

Why Families Seek Notarial Assistance

Families typically engage a notary for one of four reasons:

1. **Transfer or Assignment of Burial Spaces**

   A cemetery space may be transferred by an instrument establishing the new owner of the **right of interment.** While burial spaces are not treated as full ownership interests in the traditional sense, Louisiana law recognizes a transferable right to control interment in a designated space. The notary may prepare or authenticate a transfer, assignment, or waiver of burial rights. Often, these transfers are accomplished through a private sale, but sometimes they are done through an Act of Donation, which requires Authentic Form.

2. **Confirmation of Authority After Death**

   When burial rights are unclear – for example, when the recorded **owner of burial rights** of a space is deceased or when multiple heirs claim authority – families may seek a notary to document the chain of authority by affidavit or Authentic Act.

3. **Consent to Disinter or Reinter Remains**

   Certain disinterments require written consent or judicial authorization. A notary may prepare or authenticate the consent instrument, provided all required parties participate.

4. **Documentation of Agreements with Cemeteries or Third Parties**

   Prior to burial or even installation of a memorial, cemeteries may require notarized acknowledgments or authorizations confirming who holds decision-making authority. Although Louisiana law (particularly **La. R.S. 8:812**) does not require conveyances by a Cemetery Authority to be in Authentic Form **while still retaining the character of an Authentic Act, some cemeteries still engage notaries for peace of mind** on certain conveyances.

In each of these scenarios, **the notary's value** is the ability to:

- verify identity
- confirm intent
- record authority in a clear instrument
- reduce ambiguity before conflict arises

Limits of Notarial Authority in Cemetery Matters

A notary must remain within the boundaries of **notarial authority** and avoid functions reserved for attorneys, courts, or cemetery authorities.

A Louisiana notary **may not:**

- resolve disputes among heirs or stakeholders
- interpret where succession law conflicts with family expectations
- override a cemetery's governing rules or trust obligations
- authorize disinterment when Title 8 requires a court order
- certify the identity of remains or the location of remains
- issue any directive concerning operational burial decisions

A Louisiana notary **may:**

- prepare or authenticate instruments that establish or confirm authority to act
- draft agreements to transfer or waiver of rights associated with burial spaces, either by spouses or heirs
- prepare affidavits documenting priority of authority under **La. R.S. 8:655** and **La. R.S. 8:1 et seq.**
- authenticate consents required by cemetery rules

The notary's work provides the **legal foundation upon which cemeteries act,** but does not substitute for the authority of the cemetery itself. This distinction protects the integrity of cemetery operations while enabling families to exercise rights documented through proper instruments.

The Emotional Context Does Not Expand Legal Authority

Although cemetery issues arise during times of grief, the notary's authority remains unchanged. Expressions of sympathy are human and appropriate, but the legal function of the notary does **not** expand or contract based on circumstances.

Families may attempt to present a notary with competing claims or emotional appeals. The notary must maintain neutrality and may only:

- **authenticate what is true and presented**, or
- **decline involvement** when authority cannot be established.

Notaries should be prepared to say:

"I cannot determine who is entitled to authorize burial. I may assist once the parties' authority is documented or adjudicated."

This sentence resolves many attempted overreaches into unauthorized practice of law.

When a Notary Becomes Essential

Cemetery authorities and funeral homes frequently rely on notarial instruments because:

- **burial rights lapse through generations** without clear documentation
- family members die and **do not leave declarations** on who is to be buried in extra burial spaces
- **burial spaces are acquired jointly** without a later agreement on control
- **spousal burial rights under La. R.S. 8:805** supersede succession rights of heirs
- **cremated remains complicate lineage and custody** when multiple parties claim an interest
- **cemetery rules require notarized consent** to prevent later disputes

Without notarized instruments, cemeteries and families may face:

- delayed interments
- contested burial decisions
- refusal to authorize disinterment
- future litigation over the right of interment
- uncertainty when successors seek burial decades later

Thus, the notary becomes the **neutral recorder of authority**, providing certainty that enables cemeteries to act correctly and confidently.

COMMON SITUATIONS ENCOUNTERED BY NOTARIES

Scenario	Instrument Needed	Notes
Deceased recorded owner of burial rights; heirs seek burial	Affidavit of Heirship confirming authority	Notary verifies facts presented; does not adjudicate heir disputes
Transfer of unused burial spaces	Sales Agreement or Act of Donation	Confirm spouse's vested right under **La. R.S. 8:805**
Estranged spouse opposes burial	Notarial role is limited unless spouse waives rights	Do not adjudicate disputes; parties may need counsel
Multiple heirs signing consent for disinterment	Disinterment Authorization with all required signatures	Court order required when statutory consent cannot be obtained
Cemetery requires written authorization from next of kin	Notarized Acknowledgment of Authority	Confirms priority under Title 8, but notarial act does not grant authority

This table outlines what the notary can document without exceeding authority.

Distinguishing Cemetery Rights From Real Property

Louisiana notaries trained primarily in real property law may incorrectly treat cemetery spaces as traditional ownership interests. It is not uncommon to see sales agreements or Acts of Donation to describe cemetery burial rights as real property. Such an agreement should be, but is not always, rejected by the Cemetery Authority for using incorrect language. Title 8 and case law are clear: cemetery rights are **unique**, and the terminology of ownership can be misleading.

A burial space is best understood as a **personal servitude of use, right of interment**, which may be:

- designated by the cemetery contract
- passed through succession
- waived by a written instrument
- encumbered by spousal burial rights
- bought, sold, or donated to third parties with Cemetery permission
- subject to cemetery rules and trust obligations

The notary **documents and confirms** this right – **the notary does not create it.**

Interaction With Other Disciplines

Notarial work touches, but does not replace:

Field	Authority	Notarial Interaction
Succession Law	establishes heirs and successors	Notary may prepare affidavits confirming authority to act
Property Law	defines interests; treats used burial rights as inalienable, encumbers the cemetery's property with sale of burial rights	Notary may prepare acts transferring rights
Cemetery Law	governs disposition of remains and cemetery operations	Notary documents authority; does not manage operations
Court Orders	required in specified disinterments	Notary prepares consent instruments supporting petition
Funeral Practice	funerals and interments	Notary documents authority enabling funeral arrangements

Key Statutory Touchpoints

While later chapters reference statutes in detail, notaries should be familiar with:

- **La. R.S. 8:1 et seq.** – Definitions and cemetery governance
- **La. R.S. 8:655** – Right to control disposition of remains
- **La. R.S. 8:805** – Spousal vested burial right
- **La. R.S. 8:660 - 666** – Disinterment procedures
- **La. C.C. Art. 476-497** – Property classifications (guides interpretation)

These provisions form the basis for most instruments a notary will handle in cemetery practice.

Practice Notes:
If signatures of all required parties cannot be obtained, a written instrument cannot resolve the matter. Inform parties that judicial intervention may be necessary.

A surviving spouse's burial right under **La. R.S. 8:805** applies **even if not recorded.** Confirm before notarizing any transfer instrument.

Notaries do not certify facts regarding remains or locations of burial. Those determinations belong to cemetery authorities, not notaries.

Emotional urgency does not alter legal authority. Decline when authority is unclear.

Conclusion

Cemetery law matters to notaries because **notarial instruments are essential to documenting authority** in matters concerning burial, disinterment, and transfer of cemetery rights. While the notary does not manage the cemetery or decide who may be buried, the notary provides the written certainty that allows funeral homes, cemeteries, and families to act in accordance with Louisiana law.

By understanding the boundaries of notarial authority and the unique nature of burial rights, the Louisiana notary protects families, prevents disputes, and ensures cemetery decisions rest on a solid legal foundation.

CHAPTER 2

OVERVIEW OF LOUISIANA CEMETERY LAW

Louisiana cemetery law forms a distinct regulatory environment separate from traditional real property and succession law. Understanding its structure enables the notary to correctly cite the controlling statutory authority when drafting or authenticating documents. This chapter provides a working orientation to the **statutes, regulations, and definitions** that directly affect notarial practice.

The objective is not exhaustive commentary, but a **functional roadmap:**

Where to begin, what controls, and how the law is organized when a family asks, "Who can sign?"

This is probably one of the most important moments in cemetery matters. When a death occurs, often families are at a loss to determine who is considered the proper next of kin and who should handle arrangements. This is often true when both parents are deceased, and children must decide which, or all of them, will make decisions. The notary's job frequently entails helping centralize authority when siblings want one of them to be "be in charge". Knowing the law and how to proceed is essential for the notary in this moment.

Sources of Louisiana Cemetery Law

Louisiana cemetery law rests on five primary sources:

1. **Louisiana Revised Statutes, Title 8 – Cemeteries**
2. **Louisiana Administrative Code (LAC), Title 46, Part XIII – Cemetery Board Rules**
3. **Louisiana Civil Code – property classification, succession, obligations**
4. **Judicial decisions** interpreting Title 8, succession authority, and burial rights
5. **Cemetery-specific contracts, acts, and governing documents**

Each source affects notarial work differently.

Source	Function	Notarial Relevance
Title 8, LRS	Governs cemeteries, disposition of remains, disinterment	Determines who can authorize an action
LAC Title 46	Implements Board rules and compliance	Affects cemetery procedures requiring notarial instruments, but does not have the force of a legislative act
Civil Code	Provides classification and succession framework	Guides interpretation of burial rights
Case Law	Resolves conflicts or ambiguity	Notaries must avoid contradicting binding precedent
Cemetery Rules	Operational requirements per cemetery	Notarial documents must align with cemetery policies

Organization of Title 8

Title 8 is structured in **Parts I–X**, but most notarial interactions involve three areas:

Section	Coverage	Notarial Relevance
Part I – General Provisions (8:1–8:2)	Definitions	Precise meaning of "cemetery space," "interment," "remains"
Part II – Disposition of Human Remains (8:651–8:666)	Authority to control, disinterment procedures	Determines signing authority and when court action is required
Part III – Cemetery Companies & Trusts	Operational requirements	Impacts transfers where perpetual-care rules apply

Additional provisions occasionally arise in notarial practice, particularly where cemetery companies operate under rules requiring **written, notarized instruments** to validate transfers or authority.

Core Definitions Relevant to Notaries

Title 8 contains definitions that appear simple but have **critical legal consequences**. The most important aspects of notarial drafting include:

- **Interment (La. R.S. 8:1(14))** – the disposition of human remains by burial, entombment, inurnment, or placement in a niche. Notaries document authority to perform or consent to interment; understanding the term prevents unintended overreach.

Cemetery Space (La. R.S. 8:1(4)) – a grave, crypt, vault, or niche intended for interment. This conveys the correct **unit of right** being transferred or relinquished.

- **Right of Interment** *(defined through usage and case law)* – the legally cognizable right for someone to be buried in a space or determine whose remains may be placed in a cemetery space. Notaries document this right, but do not create it.
- **Remains (La. R.S. 8:1(12))** – includes both full human bodies and cremated remains. This affects disinterment consent requirements.
- **Perpetual Care** *(Title 8, Subpart D)* – funds held in trust for maintenance. Certain transfers cannot violate perpetual-care requirements imposed by cemetery contracts.

PRACTICE NOTE:
Use statutory terminology in notarial instruments wherever possible. Avoid colloquial substitutions, such as "plot ownership," unless they are clearly defined in the instrument.

AUTHORITY TO CONTROL DISPOSITION OF REMAINS

La. R.S. 8:655(A) establishes the priority of authority to control disposition.

The notary does not determine the winner of a dispute – the notary **documents consent or lack of consent** based on the statutory hierarchy.

Simplified order (for reference during drafting):

1. Designated agent under written directive. This is done through a Notarial Declaration or through a Notarial Will.
2. Surviving spouse (unless either party filed for divorce at time of death)
3. Majority of adult children
4. Majority of grandchildren
5. Surviving parents
6. Majority of surviving adult siblings
7. Next degrees of kin, in descending order

> **PRACTICE NOTE:**
> The notary must confirm the **category of authority,** not the underlying family dynamics. Decline involvement when multiple parties claim priority without agreement.

SPOUSAL BURIAL RIGHTS – LA. R.S. 8:805

La. R.S. 8:805 establishes a **vested right of interment** for the surviving spouse in any unused cemetery space purchased by the deceased. This right exists **even when the space is not in the spouse's name, as cemetery rights are subject to the state's laws concerning community property** (see **La. R.S. 8:803** below)

> **§ 803. Descent of title to cemetery space**
> Except as otherwise provided in this Chapter, every right of interment and Cemetery space shall be subject to the laws of this state pertaining to community property, inheritance, including but not limited to the laws of intestacy, donations *inter vivos* and *mortis causa*, and successions. Heirs must provide proof of succession or an affidavit of heirship to exercise rights.

Implications for notarial practice:

- A transfer of cemetery spaces **does not extinguish spousal burial rights** unless the spouse clearly waives them or is a signatory to the transfer. In either case, the spouse's consent to the transfer must be explicit.
- A notary should **inquire about marital status** before preparing a transfer instrument. The importance here is not only the current marital status but **also the marital status at the time of purchase,** even if a divorce has taken place, unless partitioned as part of the divorce, the burial rights in the space(s) are owned in indivision.
- Failure to consider **La. R.S. 8:805** may result in a transfer that is **legally invalid.**

> **PRACTICE NOTE:**
> If a space was purchased by two spouses jointly, assume the surviving spouse retains interment rights **unless a written waiver of rights exists.** Spousal rights refer to the spouse at the time the rights were purchased and **do not extinguish** unless partitioned as part of the divorce proceedings or through a separate notarized instrument.

DISINTERMENT AND REINTERMENT — COURT OR CONSENT

La. R.S. 8:660 – 8:666 govern disinterment. From a notarial standpoint, the primary question is:

"Can this disinterment proceed based solely on written consent, or must a court order be obtained?"

General rules:

- **If all required persons consent in writing → notarized consent may suffice.**
- **If required consents cannot be obtained → judicial authorization in the form of a court order is required.**

Notarial decisions:

- prepare consent instruments **only when authority is clear**
- avoid drafting when any party objects or refuses to sign

PRACTICE NOTE:
A notarized consent does **not override cemetery rules and regulations.** Some cemeteries require a court order regardless of unanimous consent. The cemetery has the right to refuse permission to disinter.

INTERACTION WITH THE LOUISIANA CIVIL CODE

Title 8 does not exist independently – burial rights interface with **property and succession principles**. The Civil Code becomes relevant when:

- tracing authority through heirs
- confirming the classification of an interest in burial rights
- determining whether a transfer must occur by an Authentic Act
- clarifying obligations when multiple persons hold an interest in the same space

While **burial rights are not traditional ownership**, instruments affecting them often follow **the formalities for immovable property** to preserve clarity and prevent challenge.

> **Practice Note:**
> When in doubt, use **Authentic Form** for transfers or assignments of burial rights.

Cemetery Company Regulations – Louisiana Administrative Code

The Louisiana Cemetery Board administers operational and trust compliance through Title 46, Part XIII of the Louisiana Administrative Code (LAC). Because these are the rules of the Louisiana Cemetery Board, they do not have the weight of Legislative statutes and can, and have had, their authority challenged.

For notaries, the key takeaway is: **Notarial documents must not contradict regulatory requirements imposed on cemeteries.**

Common implications:

- cemeteries may require **notarized acknowledgments** before accepting a transfer
- cemeteries may maintain **forms controlling the designation of authority**
- trust-fund rules may **limit or condition transfers** of perpetual-care spaces
- naming conventions and recorded instruments may **differ among cemeteries**

PRACTICE NOTE:
Before drafting, confirm cemetery-specific requirements. A notarial act that conflicts with cemetery policy may be rejected administratively even if legally valid. A cemetery may also require that certain conveyances be made using its prescribed forms.

CEMETERY CONTRACTS AND RULES

Each cemetery may impose contractual requirements controlling the use and transfer of spaces. These documents do not replace Title 8 but **operate alongside it.**

When drafting:

- request the original purchase documents
- confirm recorded owners(s) of the right of interment
- identify any existing **designations, waivers of rights, or assignments, such as notarial declarations.** These documents are usually on file with the cemetery.

Notaries do not enforce cemetery rules, but they must ensure that instruments **do not contradict** them.

CASE LAW AS INTERPRETIVE AUTHORITY

Louisiana courts have clarified:

- the nature of burial rights
- the enforceability of spousal burial rights

- the limitations on transferring spaces contrary to contractual obligations
- the necessity of consent or judicial authorization when authority is contested

More information about Louisiana case law can be found in the companion volume in this series, *Louisiana Cemetery Case Law: Jurisprudence, Practical Lessons, and Title 8 in the Courts.*

PRACTICE NOTE:
If parties describe a scenario inconsistent with settled case law, decline to draft and recommend obtaining counsel. The notary does not reconcile disagreements about what the law *means.*

HIERARCHY OF AUTHORITY IN PRACTICE

In drafting or authenticating instruments, the notary follows this functional hierarchy:

1. **Statutes (Title 8)** – must be observed
2. **Administrative Code** – governs cemeteries' operational compliance
3. **Case Law** – resolves ambiguity or conflicts
4. **Cemetery Rules and Contracts** – conditions under which authority is exercised
5. **Notarial Instruments** – document authority but do not create it

This ordering prevents the notary from drafting an act that is technically valid on paper but **unenforceable in operation.**

CONCLUSION

Louisiana cemetery law is structured around **statutory authority in Title 8**, supported by regulatory rules, informed by civil law principles, and applied through case interpretation. The notary's role is to create instruments that conform to this structure, ensuring that authority is documented in a manner consistent with the law, regulations**, and cemetery policy.**

A working knowledge of these sources enables the notary to:

- confirm authority before drafting
- prevent inconsistent or unenforceable instruments
- provide clarity to families and cemeteries
- avoid unauthorized practice of law

With this foundation in place, the next chapter addresses the **unique nature of cemetery property rights** and how notaries document and transfer those rights in compliance with Louisiana law.

CHAPTER 3

UNDERSTANDING CEMETERY PROPERTY

Before a notary can draft an instrument involving cemetery spaces, the notary must understand **what is being transferred.** Unlike traditional immovable property, cemetery spaces do not function as "owned land" in the ordinary sense. Louisiana law recognizes the **right of interment** as a unique, inheritable, and transferable legal interest tied to a designated cemetery space, but subject to statutory limitations, cemetery rules, and spousal burial rights.

This chapter clarifies:

- what a cemetery space *is* in law,
- what rights attach to it,
- what can and cannot be transferred,
- and how those rights differ from conventional ownership.

The notary's work becomes most precise when **documents accurately identify the legal interest**, not a colloquial understanding of "plot ownership."

Cemetery Spaces as Property Interests

Louisiana does not define cemetery spaces as full **immovable ownership interests**, even though they relate to immovable land. Courts and statutory practice consistently treat cemetery spaces as **property rights of a special nature**, characterized by:

- **personal use**, not **possession of soil**,
- **control of interment**, not **general dominion**, and
- **transfer subject to spousal and contractual limits**, not unlimited alienation.

The cemetery continues to retain naked ownership of the land with broad authority to control its property using rules and regulations. When a right of use is sold, it no longer has perfect ownership of the land but is encumbered by the servitude of burial, analogous to a perpetual usufruct.

Key Points:

- **Consignment agreements are business instruments.** Cemetery space is **not a parcel of land** in the way a lot in a subdivision is. The purchaser acquires **a designated right of interment**, not title to the soil.
- **Rights of interment** are restricted in kind and number, such as to the burial of human remains, and limit the number of burials in a space based on the purchase agreement with the Cemetery. Only the cemetery can grant additional interment rights.

THE RIGHT OF INTERMENT

The **right of interment** is the core interest documented by notaries.

It consists of:

1. the authority for **oneself to be buried** or to **designate who may be buried** in a specific space;
2. the ability to **prevent the burial of another without consent,** subject to the law; and
3. the ability to **transfer or relinquish** that authority through a written instrument.

The right of interment:

- may pass through succession,
- may require the unanimous consent of co-owners to exercise,
- **does not extinguish spousal burial rights** under **La. R.S. 8:805**,
- and **does not give authority** contrary to cemetery rules or trust obligations.

PRACTICE NOTE:
When drafting, identify the right as **"the right of interment associated with cemetery space(s)"**, not as "ownership of plot number ___."

Ownership vs. Right of Interment – A Necessary Distinction

Families often use phrases such as "we own the plot" or "that's our family plot." The notary must translate informal language into **precise legal terminology.**

Colloquial Term	Accurate Legal Understanding
"plot ownership"	right of interment in a designated space
"own the land around the tomb"	generally false, as the ownership of the land belongs to the Cemetery itself.
"our family cemetery lot"	multiple rights of interment within a section, not land ownership
"we control the plot forever"	subject to cemetery rules, perpetual care restrictions, and **La. R.S. 8:805**

How Cemetery Spaces Are Acquired

A right of interment typically arises through one of three mechanisms:

1. **Cemetery Contract / Purchase Agreement**
   When a space is sold, the recorded purchaser becomes the party designated to authorize interment, subject to law and spousal rights. This is true unless the deed is issued in the name of another per **La. R.S. 8:801.**
2. **Succession or Inheritance**
   The right of interment may pass to the heirs upon the recorded owner's death, though the cemetery may require proof of succession authority.

3. **Transfer or Waiver of Rights**
   An owner of burial rights may **assign, transfer, or waive** rights to another person through an instrument executed before a notary.

Regardless of the acquisition method, cemetery rules determine **how authority must be documented** before action is permitted.

Co-Ownership and In-Indivision Interests

Multiple persons may hold **undivided rights of interment** in the same space or in numerous related spaces (e.g., a family crypt). This may also be done through joint purchase in co-ownership:

> **§ 806. Rights of co-owners**
> When the record title to a cemetery space or right of interment is in the names of two or more persons, each shall be considered as having a vested right therein and no conveyance or other disposition of space or right shall be recognized without the written concurrence of each record owner, but each owner shall have the right of interment in any unoccupied portion of the cemetery space at the time of death.

KEY POINTS:

- Authority to authorize burial **often requires unanimous consent.** This is true when there are multiple heirs in the same line of authority.
- Co-owners may execute **mutual waiver agreements,** such as in the form of a quitclaim deed.
- In-indivision interests complicate disinterment requests when stakeholders disagree.
- **Rights of Interment** are restricted in kind and number, such as to the burial of human remains, and limit the number of burials in a space based on the original purchase agreement with the Cemetery.

When drafting, identify whether signatures represent:

- **full transfer of interest,** or
- **a declaration permitting someone to be interred in an individual space,** leaving residual rights to the owner intact.

PRACTICE NOTE:

Where multiple adult children inherit a space after a parent's death, obtain **all signatures** unless one heir's authority has been **properly documented** through succession instruments or Authentic Acts.

Spousal Burial Rights and Their Interaction With Transfers

La. R.S. 8:805 grants a **vested right of interment** to a surviving spouse to any unused portions of burial spaces. This right:

- **exists independently of title records,**
- **is not nullified by transfer unless the spouse signs a waiver of burial rights or the transfer itself,** and
- **may not be overridden** by a notarial act that fails to consider spousal claims.

This right exists because burial rights are subject to Louisiana's community property laws. Unless there is a contractual regime, the spouse must also sign any sale or transfer of burial rights to another party (unless it is established that the burial right is the separate property of the individual named on the deed)

When preparing a transfer:

- inquire whether the transferor is **married, widowed, or divorced,**
- confirm whether the **space is separate or community property,**
- and identify whether a **waiver of spousal rights** is necessary by determining the **marital status at the time of purchase** of the burial rights.

Practice Note:

An instrument transferring burial spaces **without spousal signature** may create future conflict. When the transferor is married, **obtain the spouse's consent or waiver of burial rights** unless clearly unnecessary based on cemetery designation and law.

Transferability – What Can Be Transferred

Instruments may transfer:

- **the right of interment,**
- **control and decision-making authority,**
- **priority to authorize placement of remains**, and

Instruments **may not** transfer:

- **the cemetery's underlying land**, or
- **authority contrary to Title 8 or cemetery rules.**

A well-drafted act clarifies:

- *which rights pass,*
- *whether spousal rights persist,* and
- *what obligations remain with the cemetery.*

Waiver of Rights – What It Means in Practice

A **waiver of rights** differs from a transfer. A waiving party may waive their right to burial in favor of another family member.

Waivers of rights are typically used to:

- resolve in-indivision disputes,
- allow a single family member to manage future interments,
- clarify succession-related ambiguities,
- or **remove vested authority** that could obstruct action.

Waivers typically exist in two forms: **spousal waivers and waivers of heirs**. A written and notarized declaration relinquishing one's right to be interred in a particular space, governed by **La. R.S. 8:809 – 810**.

La. R.S. 8:809 provides that an heir, who has a right to interment in a space, may waive that right **in favor of another relative or the spouse of a relative**

> **§ 809. Waiver of right of interment**
> Any surviving spouse, parent, child, or heir having a right of interment in an interment space may waive such right in favor of any other relative or spouse of a relative of the deceased record owner. Upon such waiver, the remains of the person in whose favor the waiver is made may be interred in the interment space.

Example phrasing:
"John Doe hereby relinquishes and waives all rights and interests of interment associated with cemetery space no. ___, and acknowledges that said rights shall vest in Jane Doe in accordance with La. R.S. 8:809 and cemetery rules."

Cemetery Rules as Binding Constraints

Notarial instruments **must not contradict** cemetery contracts, rules, or trust-fund restrictions. A cemetery may:

- require its own forms,
- impose notarization requirements,
- require **proof of succession**, or
- decline to act until **spousal rights are addressed.**
- prohibit transfers to **third parties**

Notaries should request:

1. **original purchase records,**
2. **any designation or assignment on file**, and
3. **the cemetery's current transfer policy.**

> **PRACTICE NOTE:**
> Do not assure parties that a cemetery will accept an act. The cemetery's **administrative authority** governs operational acceptance.

RECORDKEEPING AND CHAIN OF AUTHORITY

A transparent **chain of authority** protects all parties. Best practice is to ensure:

- the cemetery receives **certified copies** of transfers or waivers,
- and successors retain **authenticated originals**.

Failure to maintain the chain of authority results in:

- disputes over rights decades later,
- refusal of cemeteries to authorize burial(s),
- litigation among heirs,
- and requests to courts to **re-establish authority** due to missing documentation.

Disputes – Limits of Notarial Involvement

When authority is contested, the notary's role is limited.

A notary **may:**

- identify that signatures are missing,
- confirm that spousal rights exist,
- document consent when **all parties agree**.

A notary **may not:**

- choose which heir has authority,
- interpret ambiguous succession without documentation,
- override objections through drafting,
- or authenticate inconsistent statements for opposing parties.

Practice Note:

When disagreement persists, a notary should say:
"This matter requires legal counsel or judicial resolution. I cannot document authority until it is established."
When in doubt, refer parties to the Cemetery Authority or instruct them to get a court order.

PRACTICAL DRAFTING APPROACH

Before drafting:

1. Identify the **owners(s)** of the right of interment.
2. Confirm if **spousal rights** exist under **La. R.S. 8:805.**
3. Determine whether the objective is the **transfer** or **waiver of burial rights** in favor of another.
4. Verify **cemetery-specific requirements** with the cemetery.
5. Obtain **all required signatures** to prevent future conflicts.

During drafting:

- use precise statutory terms,
- avoid broad assertions of ownership,
- clarify authority and limitations,
- and specify whether the spouse's vested right is waived or retained.

After execution:

- ensure the cemetery receives a recordable copy,
- advise parties to retain originals,
- maintain documentation in your notarial register.

Conclusion

Cemetery spaces represent **specialized property interests** centered on the **right of interment**, subject to statutory, contractual, and operational limits. Notaries document and transfer this right, but do not grant authority contrary to **Title 8 or cemetery rules and regulations.**

Correct identification of the legal interest is the foundation of all subsequent instruments.

Notaries who draft using accurate terminology and verified authority prevent conflict, delay, and litigation — and enable cemeteries to act with confidence.

CHAPTER 4

WHO HAS AUTHORITY?

Every notarial instrument involving cemetery rights requires a clear answer to the question: **"Who has authority to act?"**

Authority determines **who may consent to interment, who may authorize transfers**, and **who may approve disinterment.** A notary who proceeds without confirming authority risks creating an instrument that **cannot be acted upon** by a cemetery or may later be **challenged by heirs, spouses, or successors.**

This chapter addresses:

- statutory authority under **La. R.S. 8:655 and 8:805**,
- interaction with succession and civil law,
- spousal priority and exceptions,
- documentation requirements, and
- when a notary must decline drafting due to uncertainty or dispute.

THE CONTROLLING STATUTE – LA. R.S. 8:655

La. R.S. 8:655(A) establishes the priority of persons who possess authority to control the final disposition of remains and related decisions. A notary's role is **not to decide which party is "right"** but to confirm that the signatory **falls within the statutory priority** or derives authority from someone who does.

The priority, simplified, is as follows:

1. **A person designated under a Notarial Declaration or Notarial testament** executed by the decedent
2. **The surviving spouse**, if there is no pending petition for divorce filed by either party
3. **Majority of the decedent's surviving adult children**
4. **Majority of the decedent's surviving adult grandchildren**
5. **Surviving parents**
6. **Majority of surviving adult siblings**
7. **Next degrees of kin**, in descending order, consistent with civil law

KEY PRINCIPLE

The statute governs – personal preference expressed by relatives *after* death does not alter this hierarchy unless properly documented.

Do not confuse the authority to inter as the same as having authority over interment rights. The former controls the final disposition of the body - to decide how and where the decedent is interred. The latter controls the burial space itself and can determine who is buried in a particular burial space for which he/she has burial rights.

Authority for Disposition vs. Authority for Cemetery Rights

A critical distinction:

Authority to control disposition of remains	Authority to control the right of interment in cemetery spaces
Determines **who may authorize burial or cremation**	Determines **who may authorize the use or transfer of a cemetery space**
Governed primarily by **La. R.S. 8:655**	Governed by **Title 8, cemetery contracts, and succession**
Based on the relationship to the deceased	Based on **recorded rights, succession, and transfers**

In many cases, **the same person holds both authorities**, but not always.

Example: A child may control disposition under **La. R.S. 8:655**, while an uncle holds the recorded right of interment for a family crypt.

> **Practice Note:**
> When families state, "I'm her son," the notary must clarify **which authority they are invoking**, not assume both.

Spousal Authority – La. R.S. 8:805 and La. R.S. 8:655 Combined

Two statutes work together:

- **La. R.S. 8:655** gives the **surviving spouse** priority to control the disposition of remains absent another declaration by the decedent
- **La. R.S.8:805** grants the **surviving spouse a vested right of interment** in the unused space of the predeceased spouse.

Together, these provisions mean:

- The surviving spouse **often controls both disposition and cemetery placement**, unless
    - Either party filed for a pending divorce at the time of the decedent's death, or
    - the spouse **waives burial rights in writing** before or after death.

Common Oversight:

Notaries sometimes transfer burial spaces **without obtaining the spouse's signature**, unintentionally leaving a surviving spouse with **persisting burial rights** that conflict with the transfer.

Practice Note:

When preparing transfers involving persons who were **married at the time of purchase**, obtain the spouse's signature or execute a **waiver of spousal burial rights** unless clearly unnecessary.

SUCCESSION CONSIDERATIONS

Authority may pass through:

- **testamentary succession**,
- **intestate succession**, or
- **small succession affidavits**.

However:

- **succession determines heirs**, not authority for disposition of remains or burial decisions unless the succession judgment explicitly grants that authority.

A notary must avoid assuming that **Heirship = Authority, as the two are often** different.

Instead, the notary should document authority as follows:

- heirs may **inherit the right of interment**, but
- **the priority to authorize disposition does not always mirror succession**, and
- cemeteries may require **proof of succession** before recognizing authority to transfer spaces.

> **PRACTICE NOTE:**
> When a recorded owner is deceased, a notary may prepare an **Affidavit of Heirship for Burial Rights** to document who succeeds in the cemetery interest – but this instrument **does not override La. R.S. 8:805 or La. R.S. 8:655.**

Authority in Indivision Situations

When multiple persons inherit rights of interment:

- **unanimous consent** is required for interment decisions,
- a **mutual waiver of burial rights agreement, such as a quitclaim,** may streamline authority,
- **objections by a single co-owner** may prevent action,
- and **a court order may be necessary** if an agreement cannot be reached.

Practical Example:
Three adult children inherit a space.
Two agree to bury a sibling's ashes; one refuses.
A notarial instrument **cannot resolve this dispute** – judicial intervention is required.

> **Practice Note:**
> Drafting for less than all co-owners may create an instrument that is **facially invalid** for cemetery operations.

Authority to Transfer vs. Authority to Consent

A signer may have authority to:

- **authorize burial**, but **not transfer the space**, or
- **transfer the space** but **not authorize the burial of someone else's remains.**

Example distinctions:

Action	Statutory Basis	Authority Required
Authorize burial of remains	**La. R.S. 8:655**	Statutory priority
Authorize disinterment	**La. R.S. 8:660–666**	Consent of the required parties or a court order
Transfer cemetery spaces	**Title 8 + contracts**	Recorded owner(s) or successors
Waive spousal burial rights	**La. R.S. 8:805**	Surviving spouse

PRACTICE NOTE:

Confirm the **objective of the document** before preparing it. Many conflicts arise from drafting **the wrong instrument** for the authority that exists.

DOCUMENTATION OF AUTHORITY

A notary should document authority through:

- **affidavits of heirship for burial rights**,
- **Authentic Acts of transfer or waiver of burial rights**,
- **acknowledgments confirming spousal rights**, and
- **written designations recognized under Louisiana law.**

Best practice is to **state explicitly** the statutory basis relied upon.

Example language:
"Authority to authorize this transfer is derived from La. R.S. 8:655 and documented by the accompanying Affidavit of Heirship for Burial Rights dated____."

When the Notary Must Decline

A notary must refrain from drafting or authenticating an instrument when:

- **multiple parties claim priority** and disagree,
- **the required party refuses to sign,**
- **authority cannot be established from documentation,**
- **the family requests an interpretation of conflicting succession positions,** or
- **drafting would affect legal rights beyond notarial authority.**

Sample statement when declining:
"I cannot document authority until it is established. This matter may require legal counsel or judicial determination."

Common Authority Misconceptions

Claim	Legal Reality
"I'm the oldest child, so I decide."	Priority under **La. R.S. 8:655** requires the **majority of adult children**, not seniority.
"I paid for the space, so I control it."	Payment does **not override spousal burial rights** or succession. The person who purchases a space is not always the listed owner of burial rights in that space. The owner who controls who is or isn't buried in the space is the party listed on the deed.
"We inherited equally, so I can sign for all."	**All co-owners** must sign unless authority is otherwise documented.
"The cemetery already knows our family."	Cemeteries **require documentation** before acting – memory is not authority.
"I'm the executor, so I decide."	Executors do **not control disposition** unless designated under law.

Practice Note:
Notaries do not correct misconceptions through **legal interpretation** – they reference the statute and **document only what is clear.**

Checklist – Confirming Authority Before Drafting

Before preparing any instrument, verify:

- ✓ Who holds the **recorded right of interment**
- ✓ Whether the **recorded owner is deceased**
- ✓ Whether a **surviving spouse holds a vested right** under **La. R.S. 8:805**
- ✓ Whether **successors are unanimous** when required
- ✓ Whether **cemetery rules require additional forms**
- ✓ Whether **the objective is transfer, relinquishment, or consent**
- ✓ Whether **a court order is necessary** due to a lack of agreement

If any box is unresolved → **pause drafting.**

Conclusion

Authority is the **threshold question** in cemetery practice. Louisiana law provides a clear statutory hierarchy for the disposition of remains and a spousal right of interment that persists unless relinquished. Succession may determine who inherits rights, but **inheritance does not automatically confer decision-making authority.**

The notary must verify authority **before drafting,** decline when authority is unclear or disputed, and reference statutes precisely to ensure instruments will be accepted by cemeteries and withstand future scrutiny.

CHAPTER 5

AUTHENTIC ACTS RELATED TO CEMETERY RIGHTS

Notarial involvement in cemetery matters primarily concerns the preparation and authentication of written instruments affecting **the right of interment**, including transfers and waivers of burial rights.

Because the right of interment functions similarly to an immovable property interest and is **subject to community property, succession, and cemetery rules**, the safest and most widely accepted method of documenting these changes is through an **Authentic Act**, unless a statute or cemetery requirement clearly permits otherwise.

This chapter provides:

- when an Authentic Act is required or advisable,
- drafting principles,
- signature requirements,
- spousal considerations,
- recordability concerns,
- and structuring for operational acceptance by cemeteries.

WHY USE AN AUTHENTIC ACT?

Louisiana law does not expressly require **all** cemetery transfers to be in authentic form. However, the use of an Authentic Act achieves four objectives critical to cemetery practice:

1. **Establishes identity and intent beyond dispute**
2. **Reduces challenges by heirs or successors decades later**
3. **Meets the expectations of many cemetery authorities**
4. **Creates a durable record suitable for long-term preservation**

> **KEY PRINCIPLE**
>
> **When in doubt, use Authentic Form.** Burial records may become relevant 20–80 years after execution – clarity and formality protect future generations.

AUTHENTIC FORM DEFINED

Under Louisiana Civil Code art. 1833, an **Authentic Act** is executed in **Authentic Form** when:

- executed before a notary public, **in the presence of two competent witnesses,**
- signed by each party, each witness, and the notary,
- and **identified in a manner sufficient to establish identity** (e.g., ID reference, known to the notary, etc.).

In cemetery practice, the Authentic Act often includes:

- **full names and capacities** of all parties,
- **identification of the cemetery space(s)** with specificity,
- **statement of marital status**, and
- **clear operative language** transferring or waiving rights of interment.

WHEN AN AUTHENTIC ACT IS *REQUIRED* VS. *ADVISABLE*

Action	Minimum Form	Best Practice	Notes
Transfer of right of interment to another person via Donation	Written instrument	**Authentic act**	Preserves future enforceability
Transfer of right of interment to another person via Private sale	Written Instrument	**Authentic Act Not Required**	May be accomplished through private signature
Waiver of right of interment	Written instrument	**Authentic act**	Authentic Form as individuals typically do not give up rights
Waiver of spousal burial right under **La. R.S. 8:805**	Written instrument	**Authentic act**	Authentic Form as individuals typically do not give up rights
Consent to disinterment when all parties agree	Written consent	**Authentic act**	Some cemeteries require a court order regardless
Acknowledgment of authority to act	Notarial acknowledgment	**Varies**	Depends on cemetery requirement
Proof of heirship to cemetery rights	Affidavit	**Not necessarily authentic**	But authentication improves reliability

> **Practice Note:**
> **Transfers and spousal relinquishments** are the **most critical** instruments to execute in authentic form to avoid operational or judicial challenge.

Signatures and Capacity Requirements

The notary must ensure:

- **all parties with authority sign,**
- signatories **understand they are transferring or waiving a legal interest,**
- **capacity exists,** and
- the identity of each party is verified.

Essential signature elements for transfers:

- the **recorded owner of the right of interment,** and
- the **spouse of the owner, if spousal burial rights exist** or may exist.

If the recorded owner is deceased:

- successors may transfer rights **only after authority is documented** (see Chapter 4).

> **Practice Note:**
> **Do not draft** if any required signature is missing or disputed. A defective signature set renders an instrument **operationally invalid** regardless of form.

Identifying the Cemetery Space

Precise identification is necessary to avoid ambiguity.
A description should include:

- cemetery name,
- section, block, row, and space number where applicable,
- niche number or crypt location,
- **purchase contract reference** if available,
- and the **cemetery's internal designation,** if different from the public map.

Example description:
"Holy Family Cemetery, New Iberia, Louisiana – Plaza VIII Mausoleum, Courtyard South, Row D, Space 919, as recorded in Purchase Contract No. 1998-347 and Cemetery Records dated April 4, 1998."

Spousal Burial Rights – Inclusion in Instruments

When drafting an Authentic Act involving cemetery rights, the notary must determine whether the spouse of the transferring party holds or may hold a **vested right of interment** under **La. R.S. 8:805**.

Common drafting methods:

1. **Spousal Joinder:** spouse signs as a party, expressly transferring or acknowledging the effect.
2. **Spousal Waiver Clause:** spouse signs a waiver of vested rights now or in the future.
3. **Marital Status Clause:** if unmarried, widowed, or legally separated, this is stated.

Minimum Best Practice:
Include a clause addressing spousal status **in every transfer instrument.**

Sample clause:
"The appearing party declares that he is married to Jane Doe, and was married to same at the time of purchase, who joins herein to waive any vested right of interment under ***La. R.S. 8:805*** *in the above-described space(s)."*

DRAFTING LANGUAGE – PRECISION AND CLARITY

Essential components of cemetery-related Authentic Acts:

- **Operative verb:** "transfers," "assigns," "relinquishes," "designates," "waives," etc.
- **Subject of transfer:** "the right of interment associated with..."
- **Identification:** cemetery name and specific space
- **Conditions:** subject to cemetery rules and Title 8
- **Acknowledgment of marital status**
- **Effective date**

Avoid ambiguous phrasing such as:

- "ownership of plot"
- "full control forever"
- "family space"
  These terms lack precision and may misrepresent legal effect.

Conveyances by the Cemetery

Sales and other Conveyances of Cemetery burial rights, although they are not sales of real property, do involve an encumbrance of real property. In Louisiana, transactions involving real property typically need to be recorded with the clerk of Court and must also be an Authentic Act.

An Authentic Act is a term in the state of Louisiana for an agreement signed by the relevant parties and two witnesses before a notary public, in the case of cemetery conveyances, **La. R.S. 8:812 merely requires that the act of conveyance by the Cemetery be done on a form "prescribed by the Cemetery Authority" and, once signed by the purchaser and the Cemetery Authority, that any such conveyance is an Authentic Act as though it was passed before a notary public and two witnesses.**

> **Important:**
> **This is a notable *exception* under the law. This author knows of no other instance in which only the signatures of the purchaser and the seller qualify as an Authentic Act.**

For practical purposes, this means that only the purchaser and the seller need to sign a cemetery sales agreement, and that agreement is self-proving in a court of law. Such an act does not need to be filed in any public office (such as the clerk of Court).

§ 812. Conveyance of cemetery spaces; formality and recordation
Cemetery Authorities that own land destined as places for the interment of human remains may convey portions thereof, or cemetery spaces located therein, for interments. The acts of conveyance shall be passed under the form prescribed by the Cemetery Authority, and any acts so made shall be equally authentic and impart full proof as if passed before a notary and two witnesses. It shall not be necessary to record such instruments in any public office.

This statute **creates an exception** to the authentic-form rule – **but only for transfers and sales made under Title 8**, i.e., transactions between a cemetery authority and a purchaser.

APPLICATION OF LA. R.S. 8:812 TO AFFIDAVITS AND CEMETERY INSTRUMENTS

Instrument Type	Is Authentic Form Required by La. R.S. 8:812?	Notes / Reasoning
Interment Right Sale or Transfer	❌ Not required between parties	Must be **in writing**; only **acknowledgment or Authentic Form** needed if it will be **recorded** in parish conveyance records, which is not required.
Assignment of Interment Rights	❌ Not required between parties	Authentic Form recommended for evidentiary value or filing in parish conveyance records, which is not required.
Waiver of Interment Rights	✅ Yes	**Authentic Form** is required because individuals do not normally give up the rights to things. **La. C.C art. 1541.**

Instrument Type	Is Authentic Form Required by La. R.S. 8:812?	Notes / Reasoning
Dation en Paiement of Burial Space	✅ Yes	This is a *civil code dation* (**La. C.C. art. 2655**), not a mere Title 8 sale; must be authentic.
Affidavit of Heirship or Ownership for Burial Space	⚠️ Optional	May be by acknowledgment; authentic form is required only if it is to be **recorded** for notice.
Declaration or Trust Affecting Burial Space	⚠️ Usually advisable	Title 8 doesn't require authentic form, but **La. R.S. 9:1752** (Trust Code) allows either **authentic or acknowledged** form.
Servitude or Easement for Cemetery Access	✅ Yes	This is a *real servitude* under the Civil Code – must be an Authentic Act.
Designation of Burial Rights within a Family	⚠️ Not required by statute	For long-term enforceability, an authentic form is recommended.

ACTS OF DONATION AND THE REQUIRED FORM

Scenario	Governing Law	Form Required	Reasoning
Donation by Cemetery Authority to Purchaser (a Title 8 "conveyance")	**La. R.S. 8:812**	Writing suffices; Authentic Act is not required unless recorded	Treated as a sale or conveyance under Title 8
Donation by Private Owner of Interment Right to Another Person (family or third party)	**La. C.C. art. 1536**	**Authentic Act required**	Donations *inter vivos* of rights require an Authentic act when Cemetery is not a party.

PRACTICAL SUMMARY

Purpose	Authentic Form Required	Citation
Cemetery ↔ Purchaser	❌ No	Covered by **La, R.S. 8:812(A)**; written signature sufficient.
Private ↔ Private Transfer	❌ No	**La. C.C. art. 1839** allows transactions to be passed by Authentic Act or under private signature.
Donation / Dation / Partition	✅ Yes	Governed by **La. C.C. arts. 1536, 2655, 807.**

Key Points:

La. R.S. 8:812 creates a *limited exception* to Louisiana's general authentic-act rule: a cemetery deed, sale, or transfer is valid between the cemetery authority and the purchaser even without authentic form, but an authentic or acknowledged form is still **required for recordation** and **third-party protection.**

Recording and Retention

Unlike land transfers, cemetery instruments are not filed with the clerk of court **unless the cemetery requires it** or the parties choose to preserve recordation for clarity. However, according to Title 8 **The Cemetery is the recording authority. ALL CONVEYANCES, whether private acts or not, MUST BE RECORDED WITH THE CEMETERY AUTHORITY FOR VALIDITY.** Best practice for notaries:

- provide the **cemetery with a certified copy of the act,**
- provide each party with an **executed and signed copy,**
- retain **proof of delivery** to the cemetery, or
- execute a statement that **relieves the notary** of all responsibility for recording the signed instrument with the Cemetery if the Notary will not be the filing party.

Practice Note:

Never assume the cemetery will permanently retain documents. Files may be lost over decades – redundancy protects future authority.

Use of Acknowledgments in Cemetery Practice

Notarial acknowledgments are used when:

- a cemetery requires **confirmation of authority**, not transfer,
- a funeral home requests **verification of authority to consent**, or
- an institution needs **proof of signature validity**.

Acknowledgments **do not transfer rights** – they only affirm identity and execution.

If authority needs to be **granted or waived**, use an **Authentic Act**, not an acknowledgment.

Drafting to Avoid Future Disputes

An Authentic Act should anticipate that:

- successors may challenge,
- documentation may resurface decades later,
- the cemetery may require clarity beyond ordinary standards,
- legal interpretations may evolve.

Draft with long-term clarity. Families rarely review these instruments immediately – **they review them when needed most**, often years later, during burial planning or disputes.

Template Structure for Cemetery Transfer Instruments

A reliable internal structure is as follows:

1. **Title** – "Transfer of Right of Interment"
2. **Appearances / Parties & Identifications (included marital status and history as part of the appearance clause)**
3. **Recitals** – background and purpose
4. **Operative Clause** – transfer or waiver language
5. **Description of Cemetery Space(s).**
6. **Conditions & Limitations**
7. **Delivery and Effectiveness**
8. **Signature Blocks**
9. **Witness Signature Blocks (Authentic Acts)**
10. **Notarial Authentication Clause**

Practice Note:
Chapters 12–15 will provide example language in context; Part IV of the book will provide forms.

When Not to Draft

Do **not** draft an Authentic Act when:

- **authority is disputed or unconfirmed**,
- **spousal rights have not been resolved**,
- **cemetery rules require additional documents first**,
- **the signer requests language that exceeds legal authority**,
- **the objective is unclear**, or
- the family seeks to **circumvent a required court order** for disinterment.

Sample statement when declining:
"Authority must be established or resolved before documentation can proceed. I cannot prepare an instrument until that is complete."

Conclusion

The Authentic Act remains the **gold standard instrument** for documenting changes to the right of interment in a manner that is reliable, durable, and acceptable for cemetery operations.

Its precise drafting preserves the chain of authority, protects against future challenges, and ensures that subsequent chapters – which address **transfers, assignments, relinquishments, affidavits, and disinterment consents** – rest on a solid foundation.

CHAPTER 6

TRANSFERS, ASSIGNMENTS, & MUTUAL WAIVER AGREEMENTS

Once authority is confirmed (Chapter 4) and the form of the act is selected (Chapter 5), the notary must determine **which type of instrument is appropriate** for the family's objective.

Cemetery matters commonly require one of three instruments:

1. **Transfer** – moves the right of interment to a new owner
2. **Assignment** – designates authority or future interment priority without full transfer of ownership
3. **Mutual waiver of burial rights** – resolves shared authority by allowing one or more parties to relinquish their rights to another

Each instrument has distinct drafting requirements and effects. The notary must select the correct instrument before drafting, as **misuse creates operational problems, disputes among heirs, or confusion for cemeteries decades later.**

DISTINGUISHING THE INSTRUMENTS

Instrument Type	Primary Effect	Who Signs?	When Used
Transfer	Right of interment moves to a new owner	Current owners(s) + spouse if applicable	Selling, gifting, or transferring authority to a person outside shared inheritance*
Assignment / Notarial Declaration	Authority to be buried delegated or designated, without divesting the owner of ownership of the rights	Owner(s) + spouse if applicable	Granting priority or authority without full divestiture
Mutual Waivers of Burial Rights	One or more co-owners relinquish rights to another party	All co-owners + spouses	Resolving in indivision rights; consolidating authority (Quitclaim or Partition)

***When gifting, draft the transfer as an Act of Donation, which is always done in Authentic Form.**

Practice Rule:
Transfers divest. Assignments/Declarations designate. Waivers give up rights. The notary's task is to identify which goal applies before drafting.

Transfers – Full Change of Owner of Rights

Definition:
A transfer completely divests the current owner(s) of the right of interment and vests that right in another person or entity, subject to Title 8 and cemetery rules.

Essential drafting elements:

- identification of the transferring party
- identification of the receiving party
- description of cemetery space
- **marital status and waiver clause if applicable**
- effective date
- delivery of execution copy to the cemetery

Practical Purpose:
Transfers are used when the right is **moving out of the original lineage or joint ownership structure.**

Common Transfer Scenarios

- A family sells unused spaces to another family
- A recorded owner gifts a space to a relative
- Rights move from joint family ownership to a single individual via purchase

In all scenarios:

- **the transferor loses all ownership (control) of burial rights**, and
- **the cemetery will require the instrument** before acting on future decisions.

Spousal Considerations in Transfers

Because burial rights are subject to community property rules, spouses must sign an agreement when ownership of burial rights is transferred, especially when there is more than one burial right, as the spouse automatically has a vested right of interment in that space. To resolve these issues, the Notary has the following options:

1. **Declaration of unmarried status**
2. **Spouse acts as a signatory on the transfer**
3. **Statement of spousal predecease or legal divorce with partition of cemetery space**
4. **Previously executed Quitclaim Deed or Act of Partition**

> **Minimum Best Practice:**
> *Always address marital status in transfer instruments, regardless of cemetery policy.*

Assignments – Designating Burial Authority Without Divestiture

Definition:

An assignment does **not** divest the assigning party of the ownership of a right of interment. Instead, it **grants or confirms another person's authority** to be interred within the designated space. Assignments are accomplished through Notarial Declarations or Notarial Testaments

Assignments are useful when:

- an owner wishes to **clarify who may be interred in any extra available spaces** while retaining ultimate interest
- A parent wants to **designate which individuals are buried in which spaces**
- A family seeks to **simplify future action** without losing ownership
- An owner wishes to retain the right to change who is buried in which space while they are still alive.

Key Distinction

Assignments designate authority to be buried; transfers change ownership of rights.

Assignment vs. Power of Attorney

Families may request a **power of attorney** to allow someone to handle cemetery matters. However:

- Powers of attorney **terminate at death,**
- **Titles 8 and 9** limit their effect on burial rights, and
- **cemetery matters arise after death**, when POA authority no longer exists.

Correct Approach:

Use **an assignment** in the form of a **Notarial Declaration or Notarial Testament** recognized under Title 8 to document future burial designation.

Drafting Considerations for Assignments

An effective assignment:

- references **the right of interment**, not general control of "property"
- **does not purport to transfer ownership**
- clarifies **that the individual is permitted to be buried in a designated space**
- identifies **spousal rights**, if affected

Practice Note:

Avoid language that grants "ownership" in an assignment. Such phrasing may unintentionally convert the instrument into a transfer.

Mutual Waiver Agreements – Consolidating Authority

Definition:
A mutual waiver agreement occurs when **multiple co-owners** relinquish their rights of interment to **a designated person, or when all but one waive their** authority to prevent operational impasses.

These agreements are common when:

- siblings or heirs inherit a single family space
- former spouses own a space or spaces in indivision and wish to partition their space ownership
- only one family member is willing to make future burial decisions
- disinterment or reinterment may be required in the future
- **cemeteries require a single point of authority** before acting

Purpose:
Clarity for future decisions – eliminating potential disputes by consolidating ownership now.

Required Signatures for Mutual Waivers of Interment

- **All current co-owners** of the right of interment (or successors)
- **Spouses of each relinquishing party,** when spousal burial rights exist
- **Recipient of the consolidated authority** (though not required, customary)

PRACTICE NOTE:
If even **one** co-owner refuses to sign, the notary **cannot consolidate ownership of burial rights** solely through drafting.

INSTRUMENTS TO USE

There are two primary instruments for accomplishing a mutual waiver of rights - a Quitclaim Deed or a Partition of Burial Rights in Indivision. Both instruments essentially achieve the same purpose. It is important to note that these instruments are widely used whenever a couple divorces and the burial rights they purchased in indivision are not included in the partitioned assets in the divorce. These instruments allow parties to partition rights in space so that either party can sell or transfer to another party.

AVOIDING IMPROPER INSTRUMENT SELECTION

Do **not:**

- use an assignment to divest ownership,
- use a transfer to allow someone to be buried in a space without the intent of retaining ownership,
- use a waiver of rights when heirs **disagree,** and court action is required,
- draft any instrument **without an explicit spousal acknowledgement,**
- suggest that a cemetery must accept an instrument **contrary to its rules.**

Decline if unclear:
"This matter requires clarification of the objective and authority before I can draft."

Instrument Effectiveness – Record, Deliver, Confirm

After execution, the notary must ensure:

1. **copies delivered to the cemetery** (or divest himself of this responsibility in the instrument)
2. **copies delivered to successors** if known
3. **parties are advised to maintain copies with estate documents**

> **Best Practice:**
> *Confirm acceptance by the cemetery once delivered.* Some cemeteries require internal approval before taking action.

Long-Term Validity Considerations

Cemetery decisions may arise decades later. Drafting should anticipate:

- death of the parties who signed,
- turnover of cemetery administration,
- potential relocation of records,
- multiple future interments in a single space,
- future requests for disinterment.

Practice Rule:
Presume your document will be consulted when all signatories are deceased.

DRAFTING EXAMPLE DISTINCTIONS (CONCEPTUAL)

Below are **conceptual, not final form templates** – complete forms available in *The Louisiana Cemetery Forms Book.*

Transfer (conceptual)

Whereas the assignor is the lawful owner/heir of interment rights in space(s) designated in the books of Holy Family Cemetery as Plaza VII Mausoleum, Courtyard North, Row B, 101

WHEREAS the ASSIGNOR desires to transfer and assign all rights, title, and interest in the above-described cemetery space(s) to the ASSIGNEES.

NOW, THEREFORE, for and in consideration of the Terms and Conditions below, the ASSIGNOR hereby transfers, conveys, and assigns all right, title, and interest in and to the above-described cemetery spaces(s) to the ASSIGNEE, their successors, and assigns, to have and hold forever.

Assignment (conceptual – In Affidavit)

AFFIANT hereby designates that the following persons are permitted to be interred in said burial spaces, one person per space, unless otherwise permitted by CEMETERY Rules and Regulations:

BURIAL SPACE NO. 1 shall be reserved for ***Jane Doe***

BURIAL SPACE NO. 2 shall be reserved for ***John Doe***

BURIAL SPACE NO. 3 shall be reserved ***for*** **Sarah Doe**

Mutual Waiver (conceptual)

Quitclaim by VENDOR: *VENDOR does hereby remise, release, quitclaim, and forever convey unto VENDEE all right, title, and interest in and to Cemetery Space 504C, together with all privileges and appurtenances thereunto belonging or in anywise appertaining.*

Quitclaim by VENDEE: *VENDEE does hereby remise, release, quitclaim, and forever convey unto VENDOR all right, title, and interest in and to Cemetery 506C, together*

FULLY DRAFTED FORMS WITH CLAUSES AVAILABLE IN THE LOUISIANA CEMETERY FORMS BOOK

Conclusion

Transfers, assignments, and mutual waiver agreements provide the **structural tools** that allow families to document authority in a way that aligns with Louisiana law, cemetery rules, and future operational needs.

- **Transfers** divest and replace owners
- **Assignments** designate non-owner burials in particular spaces
- **Mutual waivers** resolve inherited complexity when spaces are owned in indivision by partitioning spaces

The notary must choose the correct instrument based on **intent**, confirm **authority**, document **spousal rights**, and draft in authentic form to preserve long-term enforceability.

CHAPTER 7

AFFIDAVIT OF HEIRSHIP OF BURIAL RIGHTS

An **Affidavit of Heirship of Burial Rights** documents which individuals succeed to the **right of interment** when the recorded owner is deceased, and succession has not yet clarified authority.

It is **not** a succession judgment, **a transfer, or** an adjudication of disputed claims.

Its purpose is to:

1. identify successors based on facts presented to the affiant,
2. provide a written record of **who the cemetery may reasonably treat as successors**,
3. enable subsequent drafting of **transfers, assignments, or relinquishments**, and
4. document authority **without interpreting law or resolving disagreements**.

KEY LIMITATION:
The affidavit **does not create rights** – it records **facts and claims of descent** that explain who holds the cemetery rights **until proven otherwise**.

When This Affidavit Is Used

Notaries may prepare or authenticate this affidavit when:

- the recorded owner of a cemetery space is deceased, and
- successors need to **document their relationship** to manage future interments or transfers of other spaces, and
- **no judicial determination of authority exists**, and
- **all successors agree on the factual statements.**

Affidavits are appropriate:

- before drafting **mutual waivers of burial rights** (Chapter 6)
- before transferring rights inherited through multiple heirs
- when a cemetery requires **proof of succession** to update its records
- when **no dispute exists**, but the cemetery cannot proceed without documentation

> **Practice Note:**
> If heirs **disagree** about factual lineage or authority, **an affidavit cannot resolve the conflict** – court action is required.

Evidentiary Weight of the Affidavit

The **evidentiary value** of an affidavit of heirship is:

- **limited**, but
- **sufficient** for administrative cemetery actions when unchallenged.

It functions as:

- a factual representation made under oath,
- accepted by cemeteries as proof of successor authority **unless contested**, and
- a basis for *future instruments* confirming or transferring authority.

It **does not:**

- bind courts in litigation,
- replace a notarial will, succession judgment, or court order,
- negate spousal rights under **La. R.S. 8:805**,
- override the statutory hierarchy of **La. R.S. 8:655**.

> **PRACTICAL TRUTH:**
> Cemeteries routinely rely on affidavits **to avoid requiring families to open a succession, unless there is conflict or ambiguity.**

WHO SIGNS THE AFFIDAVIT

There are **two signature categories:**

1. **Affiant(s)** – persons with knowledge of lineage and facts regarding the deceased owner
2. **Notary** – authenticating the affiant's signature and oath

Affiants may be:

- the successor,
- a relative familiar with family history,
- or **at least one disinterested but informed person**, depending on cemetery policy.

§ 804. Affidavit as authorization
In the absence of a formal judgment of possession in the succession of the record owner of a cemetery space or right of interment, an affidavit by a disinterested but informed person of the facts setting forth the fact of the death of the record owner and identifying the spouse and legal heirs of the decedent shall be complete and sufficient authorization for a Cemetery Authority to permit the use of any unoccupied portion of a cemetery space by the person or persons entitled to the use thereof.

NOTARIAL ROLE:
The notary **does not certify the truth of lineage** – the notary certifies the **oath and identity** of the affiant. Apply rules consistently and reasonably **(La. R.S. 8:308)**.

WHAT THE AFFIDAVIT MAY STATE

An affidavit may lawfully state:

- the recorded owner's name and date of death
- familial relationships (spouse, children, siblings, etc.)
- that the owner **died intestate**, to the affiant's knowledge
- the identity of **surviving heirs**
- whether **any heirs predeceased** and left children
- the existence or absence of a surviving spouse
- whether the spouse **has waived burial rights**
- that **no dispute currently exists** among successors
- that successors **agree on who may act** for burial purposes

These statements are **factual assertions**, not legal conclusions.

WHAT THE AFFIDAVIT MAY NOT STATE

The affidavit must **not**:

- declare **legal interpretation** of succession
- resolve disputes between heirs
- override or extinguish **spousal rights under La. R.S. 8:805**
- assert **ownership of land**
- state that a successor's authority is **exclusive**, unless documented elsewhere
- assign, transfer, or waive rights
- act as a substitute for a **court judgment** when required

PRACTICE NOTE:
The affidavit is a **record of facts**, not a **vehicle for legal consequences** beyond documenting those facts.

Avoiding Unauthorized Practice of Law

The affidavit must not:

- interpret intestacy law,
- allocate rights among heirs,
- resolve priority under **La. R.S. 8:655**,
- or assert **how the affidavit affects legal rights**.

Permissible phrasing:
"Affiant states that, to the best of affiant's knowledge, the decedent was survived by the following heirs..."

Impermissible phrasing:
"These heirs are the legal owners of the space."
(improper legal conclusion – may only be adjudicated or established through proper instruments)

Order of Information – Recommended Structure

Best practice structure:

1. **Title**
2. **Affiant Appearance clause (including marital history)**
3. **Affiant Relationship / Knowledge Basis**
4. **Recorded Owner Identification**
5. **Date of Death**
6. **Marital Status at Death**
   (critical for **La. R.S. 8:805** implications)
7. **List of Surviving Heirs**
8. **Status of Predeceased Heirs**
9. **Statement of No Known Disputes**
10. **Statement of Purpose**
    (to document successor claims for cemetery administrative use)
11. **Affiant Signature Under Oath**
12. **Notarial Jurat and Authentication**

This structure avoids interpretation and maintains legal precision.

Spousal Rights and the Affidavit

The affidavit must:

- **recognize** spousal burial rights if they exist,
- **not claim to override** them,
- and **not certify waiver of spousal rights** unless the **spouse signs a separate Authentic Act.**

Recommended phrasing:

"Affiant states that the decedent was survived by a spouse, Jane Doe. Affiant does not attest to the effect of spousal rights under La. R.S. 8:805."

This preserves accuracy **without interpreting the law.**

CEMETERY ACCEPTANCE AND PRACTICAL LIMITATIONS

Cemeteries may:

- rely on affidavits,
- require multiple disinterested affiants, although the law only requires one,
- require additional documentation (death certificate, purchase contract, etc.),
- or require **successors to execute a subsequent transfer or relinquishment.**

PRACTICE NOTE:
Never assure a family that an affidavit will be accepted before the cemetery reviews it.

USING AN AFFIDAVIT BEFORE DRAFTING SUBSEQUENT ACTS

Affidavits often precede:

- **mutual waiver of rights agreements** (such as a quitclaim)
- **transfers among successors,**
- **assignments of burial spaces,**
- or **consents for disinterment.**

The affidavit provides **factual lineage** so the notary may draft the correct subsequent instrument.

CHECKLIST – BEFORE PREPARING AN AFFIDAVIT

Confirm:

- ✓ recorded owner deceased
- ✓ identity of spouse at death
- ✓ list of surviving descendants or heirs
- ✓ no known disputes
- ✓ affiant(s) have knowledge
- ✓ cemetery does not require additional documents first

If any are unchecked, **pause and verify before drafting.**

Sample Declarative Statements (Conceptual)

(These are not complete forms — complete forms are provided in *The Louisiana Cemetery Forms Book*)

Lineage Identification
"Affiant states that John Doe died on March 2, 2019, and was survived by the following children..."

No Dispute
"Affiant states that affiant is not aware of any dispute among successors regarding authority to act for cemetery purposes."

Purpose
"This affidavit is executed to document the identity of successors for cemetery administrative purposes and does not transfer or assign rights."

These maintain clarity without legal conclusions.

Conclusion

The Affidavit of Heirship for Burial Rights documents **factual succession** to cemetery rights, enabling cemeteries to act and notaries to prepare subsequent instruments.

It **does not adjudicate disputes, transfer rights, or override spousal claims.** Properly drafted, it becomes the factual backbone of transfers, relinquishments, and assignments that follow.

CHAPTER 8

CONSIGNMENT AGREEMENTS AND ACKNOWLEDGMENT

Cemeteries, funeral homes, and monument companies often require **written consignment agreements** when merchandise (markers, vaults, urns, memorials) is supplied or installed at a cemetery. These agreements protect **trust-fund compliance**, inventory, delivery, and installation requirements under both **Title 8** and **cemetery rules**.

The notary's role is **not** to negotiate, draft, or modify the commercial terms, but to:

1. **authenticate signatures**,
2. **confirm identity and authority**, and
3. **acknowledge execution** when the cemetery requires notarization as a condition of acceptance.

KEY PRINCIPLE:
Consignment agreements are business instruments. The notary confirms signatures — the notary does not certify commercial terms.

What a Consignment Agreement Is

For cemetery practice, a **consignment agreement:**

- documents that merchandise is supplied to a cemetery or family,
- sets terms for delivery, installation, and return if unused,
- acknowledges **pricing, liability, and trust-fund obligations** (if applicable),
- and provides clarity on **who may authorize placement** of the item.

Consignment agreements vary widely among cemeteries, but generally establish:

- the **party providing merchandise**,
- the **party responsible for payment**,
- and the **rules for placement or installation** within the cemetery.

Why Cemeteries Use Consignment Agreements

Reasons include:

- ensuring **perpetual care trust funds are not improperly bypassed**,
- confirming **installation standards** for safety and uniformity,
- documenting **who may authorize placement** in a burial space,
- avoiding **liability for unapproved work**,
- indicates who has the **authority** to order and choose a monument, and
- maintaining **consistent records for future cemetery administration.**

Practical Effect:
Cemeteries may **refuse installation** of memorials or vaults without a properly executed consignment acknowledgment.

NOTARIAL ROLE IN CONSIGNMENT AGREEMENTS

The notary's lawful duties are narrow:

- verify the **identity of the signer**,
- confirm **execution of the document**,
- complete the **acknowledgment**, and
- **authenticate signatures** when an Authentic Act is requested.

The notary does **not:**

- review pricing,
- interpret trust-fund provisions,
- confirm merchandise delivery,
- certify compliance with cemetery rules,
- or resolve authority disputes regarding placement.

PRACTICE NOTE:
Families often attempt to draw the notary into **commercial disagreements** ("They overcharged us," "We don't like this stone"). These issues are **outside the notarial authority** and must not be addressed in drafting or acknowledgment.

When an Acknowledgment Is Required

An acknowledgment is typically required when:

- the **cemetery mandates notarization** for installation approval,
- merchandise is **placed on consignment** until paid in full,
- **multiple successors** must confirm authority before placement, or
- memorial work is performed by **third parties** who are not cemetery employees.

Cemeteries may also require notarization to:

- prevent unauthorized removal or replacement,
- avoid disputes among heirs,
- enforce contractual liability for installation damage.

> **Practice Rule:**
> If the cemetery requires notarization, the notary completes the acknowledgment – the notary does not modify contract terms.

Signature Verification and Authority Confirmation

Before acknowledging a consignment document, the notary should confirm:

- the signer's **identity**,
- the signer's **authority to authorize placement**, if applicable,
- any **spousal rights** affecting decisions related to the space,
- and whether **the cemetery requires additional signatures**.

Examples of required additional signatures:

- a surviving spouse whose **vested burial right may be affected**,
- **multiple adult children** when successors share authority,
- a person designated by **assignment or mutual relinquishment.**

PRACTICE NOTE:
If the signer lacks authority, the notary may **acknowledge the signature**, but the cemetery **may reject the document.** The safest practice is to **verify authority before acknowledgment** to avoid operational invalidity.

INTERPRETING TERMS – WHAT NOTARIES MUST AVOID

Notaries must **not**:

- evaluate whether pricing is fair,
- confirm the authenticity of merchandise,
- guarantee installation timing,
- or interpret whether **trust-fund contributions** are required.

These actions constitute **legal or commercial interpretation**s beyond the notary's authority and may expose the notary to liability.

Acceptable statement:
"I verify the identity of the signer and acknowledge execution of the instrument."

Unacceptable statement:
"This agreement complies with trust-fund requirements."
(legal and financial certification – improper for notarial role)

How Consignment Agreements Interact With Cemetery Rules

Most agreements include or reference **cemetery installation requirements**, which may regulate:

- **foundation standards,**
- **upright memorial height and width,**
- **bronze and granite specifications,**
- **approved colors or designs,**
- **flower vase restrictions,**
- **timing of installation and removal,**
- and **seasonal placement rules.**

Notarial Limitation:
Notaries do **not** validate compliance – that is the cemetery's role.

If families ask whether their memorial "meets rules," the notary should state:

"Compliance with cemetery rules must be confirmed with the cemetery. My role is limited to acknowledging signatures."

Trust-Fund Implications – What Notaries Need to Know

Certain merchandise transactions involve **contributions to the perpetual care trust fund** under Title 8. These obligations apply to **cemeteries and merchandise providers**, not notaries.

What the notary must know:

- **trust-fund compliance cannot be waived** by notarizing a document,
- cemeteries may require notarization to **document who authorized placement**, and
- consignment agreements may be used to prevent **circumvention of trust contributions.**

> **Practice Note:**
> The notary does **not** certify trust-fund compliance – the notary confirms **execution**, not **financial validity**.

When Consignment Acknowledgments Support Transfers or Relinquishments

In some cases, a consignment acknowledgment supports **future notarial instruments**:

- A successor executes a consignment agreement **before** transferring authority.
- A family arranges installation **before** consolidating rights.
- A consignment agreement is challenged **after** a transfer due to missing signatures.

For this reason:

- **having all necessary signatures on the consignment acknowledgment protects future clarity**, and
- notaries should verify authority **before authentication**, even if not required by the cemetery.

Best Practices for Notaries Handling Consignment Documents

1. **Review the signature block first**
    - confirm all required parties appear.
2. **Ask for cemetery policy**
    - cemeteries differ; requirements vary.
3. **Confirm spousal status**
    - obtain joinder or relinquishment if necessary for future clarity.
4. **Verify authority**
    - confirm through succession affidavits or prior acts if available.
5. **Do not discuss commercial terms**
    - remain neutral and procedural.
6. **Authenticate signatures**
    - complete acknowledgment, or Authentic Act as required.
7. **Deliver documentation**
    - delivery record to the cemetery or instruct families to do so

Declining to Acknowledge – When Necessary

The notary must decline acknowledgment when:

- identity cannot be verified,
- authority is uncertain and execution could mislead the cemetery,
- the signer requests that the notary **certify commercial terms**, or
- the document is used to **circumvent cemetery rules or court requirements**.

Sample Declination Language:
"I cannot acknowledge this document until authority is established or clarified. My role is limited to confirming identity and execution."

Conclusion

Consignment agreements are **commercial instruments** used to manage merchandise installation and compliance within cemeteries. The notary's task is to:

- verify identity,
- confirm execution,
- document authority **without interpreting law or commercial terms**, and
- ensure the cemetery receives a document it can **accept operationally**.

By maintaining this limited but essential role, the notary facilitates cemetery administration **without exceeding statutory authority**.

CHAPTER 9

ACKNOWLEDGMENT OF RIGHT OF INTERMENT

An **Acknowledgment of Right of Interment** confirms that a person **holds the authority to authorize the placement of remains in a particular cemetery space.** Cemeteries also refer to this form as an **Interment Order** when related to burial. It is used primarily when the owner of burial rights in a space wishes to order the interment of a non-owner in a space at the time of death of the non-owner. While this form does not require notarization under Louisiana law, some cemeteries may require it; therefore, it is included here for a notary's convenience.

> **PRACTICE RULE:**
> **Authorizations of Right of Interment** are not required for persons listed as owners on the deed of burial rights per La. R.S. 8:710. However, the owner's right to burial is waived the moment he is buried elsewhere.

Unlike a transfer, assignment, or waiver of burial rights, this instrument **does not change rights** – it simply **records and confirms existing authority** so cemeteries may proceed with burial, installation, or administrative updates.

This chapter explains:

- why cemeteries require acknowledgments,
- when acknowledgments are appropriate,

- how they differ from transfers and affidavits,
- what a notary may lawfully document,
- and how to avoid unintentionally altering rights while confirming them.

> **KEY PRINCIPLE:**
> An acknowledgment confirms **current authority** – it does **not create, transfer, or extinguish** authority.

WHEN CEMETERIES REQUIRE ACKNOWLEDGMENT

Cemeteries commonly require an acknowledgment of the right of interment:

- **before burial**, when recorded documents are outdated,
- **before the installation of a monument or marker**, particularly in old family plots,
- **when successors seek to act**, but the authority was never documented after a death,
- **when internal cemetery records are incomplete**, requiring updated documentation,
- **when multiple siblings defer to one sibling**, but do not transfer ownership,
- **when pre-need arrangements were made**, but control documents were lost.

In these situations, cemeteries need **evidence of who can sign,** but the family may not want or need to execute a transfer.

OPERATIONAL REASON:
Cemeteries must avoid placing remains or monuments **based on informal family statements** – acknowledgments create documented certainty.

DISTINCTION BETWEEN ACKNOWLEDGMENT, TRANSFER, AND AFFIDAVIT

These instruments serve different purposes:

Instrument	Primary Function	Changes Rights?	Common Use
Transfer	Moves right to a new owner	**Yes**	Selling or gifting spaces
Waiver of Burial Rights	Waives individual's right to burial in favor of another	**Yes**	Resolving in-indivision or allows burial of another
Assignment by Declaration	Designates burial of an individual without loss of ownership	**Maybe**	Granting permission for another to be buried in a space
Affidavit of Heirship	Records factual lineage	**No**	Establishing successors
Acknowledgment of Right	Confirms existing authority	**No**	Allowing cemetery to act, such as in burial of a non-owner

PRACTICE RULE:
If the goal is **clarification**, not **change**, use an acknowledgment–not a transfer or relinquishment.

WHAT AN ACKNOWLEDGMENT MUST STATE

An acknowledgment must:

- identify the cemetery space,
- identify the person(s) recognized as holding authority,
- state **how** authority is derived (purchase, succession, relinquishment, etc.),
- state that the signer **understands and confirms** their authority,
- state what action they are undertaking, such as the burial of remains of an individual or the installation of a monument
- be executed before a notary when required by cemetery rules.

It **should not** interpret law, succession, or dispute resolution – only **confirm the authority the signer believes they hold.**

Recommended phrasing:

"Appearing party acknowledges and confirms that they hold the right of interment associated with Space ___ based on recorded purchase and succession as reflected in attached documents."

WHAT AN ACKNOWLEDGMENT <u>MUST NOT</u> DO

The acknowledgement **must not**:

- transfer any rights,
- extinguish spousal rights,
- resolve disputes,
- claim superiority over another successor,
- declare interpretation of **La. R.S. 8:805** or **La. R.S. 8:655**,
- override cemetery rules,
- or act as consent to disinterment.

Prohibited phrasing:
"This acknowledgment makes John Doe the only person with authority." (Improper – acts as transfer or adjudication.)

Permissible phrasing:
"Appearing party acknowledges they currently hold the right of interment under existing documents."

RELATIONSHIP TO SPOUSAL BURIAL RIGHTS

Acknowledgments must **recognize**, not override, spousal rights.

When authority is acknowledged **after the death of a spouse**, clarifying language is recommended:

"Appearing party acknowledges that this instrument does not extinguish or alter any vested right of interment held by any surviving spouse under La. R.S. 8:805 unless separately documented."

When acknowledging authority **while married**, a spouse's signature may be advisable to prevent future conflict.

> **Practice Note:**
> Notaries should **ask about marital status**, but **not advise** on the legal effect of spousal rights beyond confirming whether spousal rights are addressed in accompanying instruments. Remember that spousal rights pertain to the spouse at the time the burial rights were purchased, as burial rights are part of the community property regime.

Avoiding Unauthorized Practice

The acknowledgment must:

- confirm facts,
- confirm authority,
- remain neutral.

The acknowledgment **must not:**

- determine who is "legally entitled,"
- rank heirs,
- state who "should" be buried where,
- interpret statutes or case law.

Safe phrasing:
"This acknowledgment is executed to confirm authority for cemetery administrative purposes and does not transfer or adjudicate any rights."

Acknowledgments Before Burial vs. Before Monument Installation

Acknowledgments serve different operational purposes:

Use Case	Reason for Acknowledgment
Burial / Interment	Cemetery must verify the signing authority before opening a space
Monument Installation	Cemetery must confirm who may authorize placement on the space
Reinterment (same space)	Cemetery must confirm successor authority, even without transfer
Pre-need designation	Cemetery updates internal files before future need

Practice Note:
Placement of a monument often triggers disputes later if authority was never clarified. An acknowledgment reduces later challenges.

When Declining to Prepare an Acknowledgment

The notary must decline when:

- authority is unclear,
- successors disagree,
- spousal rights are disputed,
- the family attempts to **use acknowledgment as a substitute for transfer**,

- the cemetery requires **transfer**, not acknowledgment, to proceed, or
- the signer requests language that changes rights.

Sample declination language:
"I cannot prepare an acknowledgment until authority is clearly established or agreed upon. This matter may require a transfer, relinquishment, or legal counsel."

DRAFTING STRUCTURE (CONCEPTUAL)

(Not complete forms – full forms appear in *The Louisiana Cemetery Forms Book*)

1. **Title**
2. **Appearances**
3. **Purpose Clause**
4. **Statement of Authority**
5. **Identification of Space**
6. **Statement Recognizing Limitations**
7. **Statement Indicating Action to be Performed**
8. **Statement of No Known Dispute**
9. **Execution and Notarial Execution**

Conceptual purpose clause:
"This instrument acknowledges the existing authority of the undersigned to act with respect to cemetery space ___ for administrative purposes."

CEMETERY ACCEPTANCE CONSIDERATIONS

Some cemeteries:

- accept acknowledgments **as proof of authority**,
- require acknowledgments **only when no transfer is needed**,
- require acknowledgments **before internal file updates**, or
- reject acknowledgments if **conflicts or gaps exist.**

The notary should confirm:

- **cemetery policy**, and
- **whether additional documentation is required**.

PRACTICE NOTE:

The notary **cannot require a cemetery to accept** an acknowledgment. Acceptance is a cemetery's operational decision, not a legal obligation.

CONCLUSION

An **Acknowledgment of Right of Interment** is a tool for **clarifying**, not **altering**, authority. It confirms who may act **so that cemeteries can proceed**, without transferring or extinguishing rights.

Properly drafted, it fills the gap between **succession affidavits and transfers**, allowing families and cemeteries to move forward without opening succession or adjudicating disputes.

CHAPTER 10

DISINTERMENT AND REINTERMENT AUTHORIZATION

Disinterment and reinterment involve the **removal of human remains from a place of interment**, followed by transfer to the same or another location. These actions are governed by **statute, cemetery rules, and public health regulations**, and require **strict compliance** with consent requirements to avoid legal, operational, or ethical challenges.

This chapter clarifies:

- when **written consent** is sufficient,
- when a **court order is required**,
- what a notary **may and may not** document,
- how to prepare **authorization instruments** without interpreting conflict,
- and how to avoid **overstepping into legal adjudication**.

> **CORE PRINCIPLE:**
> The notary documents authority – the notary **does not grant** authority to disinter.

Statutory Foundation – La. R.S. 8:660 - 666

Louisiana law establishes:

- **consent requirements** for disinterment,
- **public health protections**,
- and circumstances requiring **judicial involvement**.

La. R.S. 8:660

Disinterment generally requires **the written consent of those persons who have the right to control disposition** under **La. R.S. 8:655 unless** a court orders otherwise.

La. R.S. 8:662 - 666

Provide additional provisions for disinterment from **abandoned cemeteries**, **public works**, or **historic relocations**, but these scenarios are beyond ordinary notarial practice and typically require government or court action.

Operational Rule:
If **all required parties** sign a **written, notarized consent**, cemeteries may proceed unless their rules require a **court order,** regardless of consent.

Consent Requirements – Who Must Sign?

Signatories needed to authorize disinterment generally match **the priority of control of disposition** under **La. R.S. 8:655**.

In practice, this means:

1. A surviving spouse, **unless either party filed a petition for divorce before death**
2. Otherwise, **a majority of the decedent's surviving adult children**
3. If no children survive, **the surviving grandchildren**
4. If no grandchildren survive, **the surviving parents**
5. If no parents, **a majority of adult siblings**
6. Further, as statute provides

> **Key Principle:**
> **Recorded right of interment ≠ authority to disinter.**
> The right to **authorize removal of remains** follows **La. R.S. 8:655**, not **title or cemetery purchase history.**

When Consent Alone Is Not Sufficient

A **court order is required** when:

- not all required parties consent,
- **a majority of heirs with authority cannot agree**
- **the identity of the required parties cannot be confirmed,**
- **conflict exists among co-equal successors,**
- **spousal burial rights remain unresolved,**

- or **cemetery rules or public health regulations require judicial oversight.**

> **PRACTICE NOTE:**
> If **all required signatures cannot be obtained,** the notary must advise that a **court order is needed.** The notary **cannot "work around" missing signatures** through drafting.

NOTARIAL INSTRUMENT – AUTHORIZATION VS. PETITION

The notarial instrument used in disinterment practice is an **Authorization for Disinterment and Reinterment.**

It is:

- a **written consent** instrument,
- executed by the **required parties,**
- acknowledged before a notary,
- and submitted to the **cemetery** or **funeral establishment** for operational action.

It is **not:**

- a petition,
- a motion to the court,
- an adjudication,
- or a legal interpretation of **La. R.S. 8:655** priority.

Boundary Statement:
"The authorization documents consent – it does not determine who is entitled to consent."

Content of a Disinterment Authorization

An effective authorization contains:

1. **Identification of the decedent**
2. **Identification of the existing place of interment**
3. **Identification of the proposed destination** (if applicable)
4. **Statement of consent** from each required party
5. **Acknowledgment that the signer understands the act**
6. **Clarification that the document does not alter cemetery ownership or rights of interment**
7. **Execution before a notary**

Optional but recommended:

- **reason** for disinterment (brief, factual)
- **affirmation of no known dispute**
- **reference to accompanying affidavits or transfers** if necessary to clarify the chain of authority

Drafting Considerations – Avoiding Legal Interpretation

Safe drafting avoids:

- interpreting spousal rights,
- asserting succession outcomes,
- ranking heirs,
- or declaring conclusively who is "legally entitled."

Permissible phrasing:
"The undersigned persons, each of whom asserts authority under La. R.S. 8:655, hereby consent to the disinterment of the remains of…."

Impermissible phrasing:
"These persons are the only legal persons entitled to consent." (Adjudication beyond notarial authority.)

Interaction With Cemetery Rules and Public Health Requirements

Even with complete notarized consent, cemeteries may:

- require **internal approvals**,
- require disinterment authorization **using the cemetery's own forms**,
- require **court orders** as policy,
- delay disinterment based on **public health**,
- or require **verification of identity and location of remains**.

> **PRACTICE NOTE:**
> The notary does **not** verify the identity of the remains or confirm the grave location – that is a cemetery function; notarial involvement begins and ends with **documentation of consent.**

SUCCESSOR CONFLICTS – DECLINING TO DRAFT

A notary must decline to prepare an authorization when:

- **successors disagree**,
- authority **cannot be confirmed,**
- a spouse **objects,**
- the signer attempts to **exclude another required party,**
- or parties request that the notary **exclude signatures to avoid a court order.**

Sample Declination Language:
"Disinterment requires consent of all required parties or judicial authorization. I cannot prepare an instrument that bypasses mandatory signatures or court review."

TRANSFERS AND RELINQUISHMENTS BEFORE AUTHORIZATION

In complex scenarios, families may execute:

- **mutual relinquishments** (Chapter 6), to consolidate authority,
- **acknowledgments** (Chapter 9), to confirm authority,

- or **affidavits of heirship** (Chapter 7), to document successors,

before executing a disinterment authorization.

However:

- **no instrument overrides the need for unanimous consent**, and
- **no transfer can eliminate a required signature without spousal relinquishment.**

> **PRACTICE NOTE:**
> Consolidate authority **first**, then **document consent.**

REINTERMENT – WHEN TREATED SEPARATELY

Many cemeteries require **separate documentation** for reinterment, even when disinterment authorization includes the destination. Reasons include:

- **different jurisdictional requirements**,
- **public health regulations** for transport,
- and **separate operational processes.**

The notary should confirm whether the cemetery requires:

- **one combined instrument**, or
- **two separate instruments:**
    - Authorization for Disinterment
    - Authorization for Reinterment

Checklist — Before Drafting Authorization

Confirm:

- ✓ identity of the decedent
- ✓ identity of the signer(s)
- ✓ spousal status at death
- ✓ complete list of successors
- ✓ unanimous consent
- ✓ cemetery requirements
- ✓ no known disputes
- ✓ proper destination documentation (if applicable)

Drafting Structure (Conceptual)

(Not full form language – complete templates appear in *The Louisiana Cemetery Forms Book*)

1. **Title** – Authorization for Disinterment and Reinterment
2. **Appearances** – Identification of signers
3. **Statement of Authority** – Derived from statute, not adjudicated
4. **Identification of Decedent and Space**
5. **Destination Clause** – Optional if reinterment is planned
6. **Consent of All Required Parties**
7. **Statement of No Known Dispute**
8. **Limitation Clause** – Does not transfer rights
9. **Execution and Acknowledgment**

Conceptual Limitation Clause:
"Nothing in this instrument shall be construed to transfer, extinguish, or modify any right of interment or spousal right under Title 8."

CONCLUSION

Disinterment authorization is among the **most delicate** forms in cemetery practice. The notary's work is limited to:

- verifying identity,
- documenting **unanimous consent**,
- drafting instruments that **confirm authority** without **interpreting the law**, and
- declining involvement when **consent is absent or disputed**, directing parties to court.

By adhering to these boundaries, the notary preserves legal integrity, operational clarity, and protection of all parties involved.

CHAPTER 11

INDIGENT AND COMMUNAL BURIAL PROGRAMS

Some cemeteries, charitable organizations, and public agencies operate **indigent burial programs** or **communal ossuary interment programs** to ensure burial or placement of cremated remains for individuals or families unable to afford traditional arrangements.

These programs require **documentation confirming eligibility and authority, but do not alter Title 8 requirements regarding consent or control over** disposition. The notary's role is limited to **authenticating signatures** or **preparing acknowledgments and affidavits** that allow the cemetery to determine whether:

- the applicant is **eligible**, and
- the applicant **has the authority to consent to the placement of the** remains in a designated charitable or communal setting.

> **KEY PRINCIPLE**
> **Program participation does not replace statutory authority.** Charity does not circumvent Title 8.

Common Program Structures

Indigent or communal burial programs are commonly administered as:

1. **Cemetery-sponsored charitable burial spaces**
2. **Municipal or parish public assistance programs**
3. **Communal ossuary or niche programs** (for cremated remains)
4. **Religious or nonprofit charitable burial initiatives**

Regardless of structure, documentation generally requires:

- **application or request form**,
- **proof of eligibility**,
- **confirmation of authority to consent**, and
- **acknowledgment of program terms**.

The notary may be involved in items **two and three**, but not **four.**

Eligibility Confirmation – Notarial Role

Cemeteries or agencies often require **proof of eligibility**, such as:

- residence criteria,
- financial eligibility,
- status as next of kin,
- absence of pre-need contractual arrangements,
- or the identity of remains when sponsorship is arranged through third parties.

The notary may authenticate signatures or affidavits, but the notary **does not determine eligibility**, review financial records, or approve or deny applications.

Permissible:
Authenticating an affidavit stating residence in the parish at the time of death.

Not permissible:
Reviewing or determining whether the signer meets the cemetery's financial criteria.

Authority for Placement – Statutory Requirements Still Apply

Even when a burial is charitable:

- **La. R.S. 8:655 controls the authority to authorize disposition,**
- **La. R.S. 8:805 controls spousal burial rights**, and
- **consent for disinterment still requires unanimous signatures or a court order.**

Charity **does not override succession authority or spousal rights.**

> **Practice Note:**
> If a cemetery provides a burial space at no cost, the **person who authorizes placement must still be the person authorized under Title 8.**

COMMUNAL OSSUARY PROGRAMS – DOCUMENTATION NEEDS

Communal ossuary interment programs for cremated remains typically require:

- verification of **identity of remains** (handled by the funeral establishment, not the notary),
- **consent of the statutory authority under La. R.S. 8:655**,
- **acknowledgment of non-retrievability or permanence** if applicable,
- **confirmation that the remains are cremated human remains**, and
- **clarification that interment in a communal setting may be irreversible** depending on program rules.

The notary's role:

- authenticate consent,
- authenticate acknowledgment of program terms,
- authenticate relinquishment of interment expectations in individual spaces **if required by the program.**

The notary does not:

- confirm cremation,
- confirm identity of remains,
- verify the representation made by the funeral establishment or cemetery.

Waivers and Releases – Limits of Notarial Involvement

Cemetery programs may require signatories to confirm understanding that:

- burial is **charitable** and may not confer ownership,
- burial in a communal setting may **not allow future disinterment**, and
- **no subsequent claims for individual markers** may be made.

The notary may authenticate signatures on such acknowledgments, but **does not advise on waiver scope**, interpret limitations, or certify enforceability.

Required Boundary Language (when asked):
"I can authenticate your signature, but I cannot advise whether these terms waive legal rights or claims."

Multiple Successors in Indigent Burials

When a burial is provided without cost, conflicts sometimes occur among successors regarding:

- whether to accept a charitable placement,
- whether remains may be placed in communal settings,
- whether the signatory has priority or authority.

The notary must **still obtain signatures of all required parties** when:

- program terms require agreement of all successors, or
- **authority to bury remains is governed by La. R.S. 8:655**, as it always is.

> **PRACTICE NOTE:**
> Charitable burial **does not reduce signature requirements.**

PROGRAM PARTICIPATION AND FUTURE TRANSFERS

Some programs permit future:

- **transfer of remains** to a private burial space,
- **purchase of individual memorialization**, or
- **transfer of cremated remains** from communal ossuary programs where retrieval is allowed.

The notary may later prepare:

- **transfer instruments** (Chapter 6),
- **authorizations** (Chapter 10),
- **acknowledgments** (Chapter 9),

but **program terms determine retrieval rights**, not the notary.

If retrieval is **not allowed**, the notary **must not draft** an instrument suggesting it is.

DECLINING TO DRAFT – RED FLAGS

The notary must decline to prepare or authenticate an instrument when:

- **program eligibility is being contested,**
- **authority is disputed,**
- a party seeks to **exclude required signatories,**
- the document is intended to **circumvent spousal burial rights,**
- the signer requests certification beyond signature and identity, or
- the party seeks **advice about the legal effect of charitable terms.**

Required Declination Language:
"I can authenticate signatures and confirm identity, but I cannot interpret eligibility or resolve authority disputes. Consent must follow Title 8."

DRAFTING STRUCTURE – CHARITABLE BURIAL ACKNOWLEDGMENT (CONCEPTUAL)

(Not complete form – full forms appear in *The Louisiana Cemetery Forms Book.*)

1. **Title** – Acknowledgment of Authority for Charitable or Communal Burial
2. **Identification of Space or Program**
3. **Statement of Authority – without legal interpretation**
4. **Statement of Eligibility (as represented by signer)**
5. **Statement Recognizing Program Limitations**
6. **Statement of No Known Dispute**

7. **Execution and Notarial Authentication**

Conceptual Purpose Clause:
"This instrument documents authority to consent to interment under the charitable burial program described herein. It does not transfer or adjudicate rights under Title 8."

Conclusion

Indigent and communal burial programs provide **charitable options**, but **do not alter statutory authority** under Title 8.
Notaries may:

- authenticate affidavits,
- authenticate consent,
- authenticate acknowledgments of program terms,

but must not:

- determine eligibility,
- interpret waiver scope,
- resolve authority disputes.

The beneficiary may change — the law does not.

CHAPTER 12

CASE SCENARIOS FOR NOTARIAL PRACTICE

Notarial practice in cemetery matters requires **structured decision analysis:**

- **What is the objective?**
- **Who has authority?**
- **What instrument is appropriate?**
- **Is drafting permissible?**
- **Is unanimous authority present or disputed?**

This chapter provides **representative case scenarios** demonstrating how to determine:

- whether drafting is appropriate,
- which instrument applies,
- and when the notary must decline involvement.

These scenarios **do not exhaust all possibilities**, but reflect the most common situations encountered by notaries working with cemeteries.

> **CORE ANALYTICAL RULE:**
> **Identify the objective → verify authority → select instrument → confirm marital status at time of purchase → draft or decline.**

SCENARIO A – TRANSFER TO A NON-HEIR

Facts:
A recorded owner wishes to transfer an unused burial space to a lifelong friend. The owner is married; the spouse is living and wishes to retain burial rights in a separate space.

Objective:
Transfer the right of interment to a non-heir.

Authority:
Recorded owner and spouse

Instrument:
Authentic Act in the form of an Act of Donation with **spousal joinder, donating the burial rights in only one space**

Reasoning:

- Transfer divests authority
- Spousal rights under **La. R.S. 8:805** must be addressed
- Cemetery will require clarity

Drafting Outcome:
Proceed.

Scenario B – Sibling Wants to "Sign for the Family"

Facts:
Four adult children inherited a space after their mother's death. One sibling wants to authorize a burial of a grandchild but requests that the others **"not be involved."**

Objective:
Authorize burial without the involvement of all successors.

Authority Analysis:

- Under **La. R.S. 8:655**, the **majority of adult children** authorize disposition
- Under inherited rights, **all successors hold authority over the space**

Instrument Needed:
Either:

1. **Mutual waiver** to consolidate authority to one sibling **before** burial; **or**
2. **Signatures of all required parties** on an acknowledgment of authority for burial, allowing the burial of a grandchild.

Outcome:
Drafting is improper unless the **majority and succession authority match.** Advise that others must sign or waive. Both the right of interment (from the parents of the grandchild) as well as signatures of all heirs are required to bury in a burial space. Both issues of disposition and right to burial in a space must be addressed.

Scenario C – Recorded Owner Deceased, No Succession

Facts:
The recorded owner of burial rights died five years ago. Cemetery records list no successor. Two adult children request documentation to allow future burial.

Objective:
Document successor authority without formal succession.

Instrument:
Affidavit of Heirship for Burial Rights
→ followed by a **waiver of one child** if only one child should control.

Outcome:
Proceed with the affidavit **if both agree on facts** and **no dispute exists**. An affidavit may also be accomplished by a disinterested but informed person when there exists a lack of judgment of succession.

Scenario D – Spouse Refuses to Sign Transfer

Facts:
A recorded owner intends to transfer rights to an adult child. The surviving spouse refuses to relinquish spousal burial rights.

Objective:
Execute transfer without spousal relinquishment.

Authority Analysis:
Spousal rights persist under **La. R.S. 8:805,** unless waived, as burial rights are part of community property.

Instrument:
A transfer is possible but ineffective if the spouse refuses to waive their rights.

Outcome:
Advise transfer cannot proceed without spousal approval. Recommend resolving the spouse's interest first.

Drafting Outcome:
Decline draft until spousal right is addressed or parties proceed knowingly with preserved spousal claim.

Scenario E – Monument Placement Without Transfer

Facts:
Children wish to install a marker on their father's grave. The recorded space owner was their mother, now deceased; no transfer occurred.

Objective:
Authorize installation without changing ownership.

Instrument:
Affidavit of Heirship if the cemetery requires documentation.

Drafting Outcome:
Proceed.

Scenario F – Assignment Misused as Transfer

Facts:
The recorded owner signs a notarized statement stating that the daughter **"owns the plot."** The daughter now attempts to resell the space.

Problem:
The instrument was titled **"Assignment of Plot Ownership,"** which was ambiguous and unclear.

Objective:
Clarify terms and authority.

Correct Instrument:
Act of Transfer, with spousal clauses as applicable. Spousal clauses are only necessary if the property is not separate.

Outcome:
Advise on the improper instrument; draft a correct transfer only if **all parties consent.**

Drafting Outcome:
Proceed with transfer; prior assignment insufficient.

Scenario G – Family Requests Disinterment "Without Contacting Brother"

Facts:
Two of three adult children want to disinter the remains of their father. Mother is deceased. The third adult child cannot be located; last heard from five years ago.

Objective:
Disinter without unanimous signatures.

Authority Analysis:
Unanimous consent not required under **La. R.S. 8:659** for disinterment. The majority of the adult children are sufficient for disinterment and reinterment.

Outcome:
Draft disinterment order noting that the decedent had three children and that the two signing children constitute the majority of the immediate heirs under **La. R.S. 8:659,** and that the third party cannot be located.

Drafting Outcome:
Draft document for cemetery.

Scenario H – Pre-Need Designation Lost

Facts:
A pre-need designation assigned burial permission to a nephew; the document cannot be located. A cemetery requires documentation of authority before burial.

Objective:
Re-document authority.

Instrument:

1. **Affidavit of Heirship** documenting successors
2. **Assignment** from all successors to the nephew **or waiver of burial rights in an available space** to nephew

Drafting Outcome:
Proceed once **all** successors confirm authority and sign.

Scenario I – Charity Burial but Authority Disputed

Facts:
Indigent burial program available. Two siblings disagree on where the mother's burial should be.

Objective:
Authorize placement without resolving disagreement.

Authority Analysis:
Charity **does not bypass La. R.S. 8:655** – both signatures required if two children remain. If there are three children, a majority is

necessary if there is no notarial declaration or notarial testament naming an individual with final disposition of the remains.

Outcome:
Authority unresolved → no instrument appropriate.

Drafting Outcome:
Decline – advise court order or settlement among successors.

Scenario J – Cemetery Requests "Legal Confirmation"

Facts:
A cemetery administrator asks the notary to sign a statement stating that a family "legally controls" the remains.

Objective:
Authenticate legal status.

Notarial Limitation:
A notary **cannot certify legal conclusions**.

Correct Approach:
Authenticate signatures on acknowledgment or affidavit → **not** certify legal interpretation.

Drafting Outcome:
Decline certification; offer acknowledgment instead.

Scenario K – Heirs Agree Informally, No Documentation

Facts:
A cemetery will not allow interment without written proof of successor authority. Heirs verbally agree.

Objective:
Provide documentation.

Instrument Sequence:

1. **Affidavit of Heirship**
2. **Acknowledgment of waiver of burial rights,** depending on intent

Drafting Outcome:
Proceed.

Scenario L – Parent Desires to Disinter and Reinter Infant Child in a New Location

Facts:
An infant child was buried in a crypt twenty years ago while the parents were married. Parents are now divorced, and the mother wishes to move the child to a new burial location. Father is unwilling to sign the disinterment/reinterment order.

Objective:
Disinterment and reinterment of a child without the father's signature.

Authority Analysis:
Unanimous consent required under **La. R.S. 8:659** for disinterment. The signature of both parents is required.

Correct Approach:
Indicate to the affiant that both parents' signatures are required to proceed.

Drafting Outcome:
Decline to draft the order of disinterment unless both parents are willing to sign.

Scenario M – Desire to "Transfer to Avoid Signatures Later"

Facts:
Successors want to transfer rights to a single sibling solely to avoid having to obtain unanimous consent later.

Objective:
Consolidate authority to reduce future disputes.

Instrument:
Waiver of burial rights by all heirs except one, followed by **Transfer**

Outcome:
Proceed if all agree.

Analytical Summary of Scenarios

Primary Issue	Correct Instrument	Decline When
Consolidating future authority	Mutual waiver of rights	Signatures incomplete
Moving rights to a new person	Transfer	Spousal rights persist. Must sign transfer agreement
Documenting successors	Affidavit of heirship	Facts disputed
Clarifying Disposition authority	Acknowledgment	Cemetery requires transfer
Disinterment	Consent of all or court order	Party objects or missing
Charitable burial	Same authority rules	Eligibility ≠ authority

Key Lessons

- **Intent determines instrument.**
- **Authority determines whether drafting may begin.**

CHAPTER 13

WHEN YOU MUST SAY NO

Notarial work in cemetery matters often confronts **requests that exceed the notary's authority**. A notary who proceeds when authority is unclear, disputed, or legally insufficient risks:

- invalid instruments,
- operational rejection by cemeteries,
- claims of unauthorized practice of law,
- civil disputes among family members,
- and undermining the chain of authority established by statute.

This chapter provides:

- **clear criteria** for declining to draft or authenticate,
- **boundary statements** that respect authority without rendering legal advice,
- and **practical refusal language** to maintain professionalism and neutrality.

> **CORE PRINCIPLE:**
> **If authority is not established or consent is incomplete, drafting must stop.**

The Primary Red Flags Requiring Declination

A notary must decline to draft or authenticate when **any** of the following are present:

1. **Authority is disputed or uncertain**
    - disagreements among successors
    - conflicting accounts of lineage
    - uncertainty regarding priority under **La. R.S. 8:655**
2. **Statutory consent is incomplete**
    - missing signatures for disinterment
    - refusal of a required party to sign
    - attempts to bypass spousal burial rights
3. **The objective is misaligned with the instrument requested**
    - assignment is requested when a transfer is needed
    - acknowledgment is requested to avoid transfer
    - affidavit requested to avoid unanimity requirements
4. **The signer asks the notary to interpret the law or adjudicate rights**
    - "Tell us who is legally in charge."
    - "Write it so the others can't object."
5. **The signer wants the notary to confirm commercial or operational terms**
    - "Say the monument company was wrong."
    - "Say the cemetery has to accept this."
6. **The signer wants to extinguish or avoid spousal burial rights** without spousal involvement

If a red flag is present → the notary must decline
Drafting into ambiguity only moves the dispute forward; it never resolves it.

Declining When Spousal Rights Are Ignored

If a required spousal signature is absent – even if **cemetery policy is silent** – the notary must proceed with caution.

Wrong approach:

"We don't need the spouse because the space is in my name."

Correct boundary:

"Spousal burial rights exist under ***La. R.S. 8:805.*** *I cannot prepare an instrument without addressing that right."*

Outcome:
If the spouse refuses or cannot be located, no instrument is appropriate unless the parties are informed that their action **will not extinguish the spousal right** and they proceed knowingly.

In most cases, decline until spousal rights are **resolved.**

Declining When Notaries Are Asked to Interpret or Apply Law

The single most common trigger of unauthorized practice risk is **interpretation.**

Requests notaries must decline:

- "Decide who has authority."
- "Say he isn't entitled to be buried there."
- "Write it so she can't come back later."

Boundary statement:
"I cannot interpret the law or declare who has authority. My role is to document authority once established, not determine it."

Declining When Disinterment Consent Is Incomplete

Situation:
Disinterment requested; a required successor refuses to sign; others want to proceed.

Notarial rule:

Refusal to sign = judicial requirement.

Declination language:

"Disinterment requires consent of the majority of required parties or a court order. I cannot draft an instrument that bypasses required signatures."

Declining When Parties Request Avoidance of Required Signatures

Common phrasing by families:

- "Just leave my brother off; he's hard to deal with."
- "Can you notarize this without telling the cemetery my sister disagrees?"
- "If you word it right, we won't need them."

Required boundary:
"I cannot prepare a document that excludes required parties. Missing signatures may invalidate the instrument, and I cannot move forward."

Declining When Objective Is Unclear or Evolving

Notaries must pause when:

- parties do not agree on the objective, **or**
- the objective changes mid-drafting.

Boundary statement:
"I need a clear objective before drafting. Once you agree on whether you intend to transfer, relinquish, or assign authority, I may proceed."

If clarity does not emerge → **decline**.

Declining When Cemetery Requirements Conflict With Requested Instrument

If the cemetery requires:

- **transfer,** but the family wants acknowledgment, or
- **spousal relinquishment,** but the spouse will not sign,

the notary must decline.

Boundary statement:
"The cemetery's operational requirements determine acceptance. I cannot prepare a document that the cemetery has already stated it will not accept."

Declining to Certify Commercial or Operational Terms

Families may request:

- certification that fees were paid,
- confirmation that the merchandise is acceptable,
- statements that a cemetery must accept certain work.

Permissible response:
"I cannot certify commercial terms. My role is limited to verifying identity and execution of signatures."

If families insist → **decline.**

Declining When Requested to "Fix" Documents Drafted Elsewhere

If a flawed or informal document exists:

- notaries may **replace** it by drafting a correct instrument,
- **not repair, explain, or interpret** the prior instrument.

Boundary statement:
"I cannot interpret this document or confirm its legal effect. If you want to correct or replace it, I can draft a new instrument once authority and intent are clear."

Declining When Asked to Guarantee Cemetery Acceptance

Prohibited request:

"If you notarize this, the cemetery has to accept it, right?"

Correct response:

"The cemetery determines acceptance. I can prepare an instrument consistent with Title 8, but I cannot guarantee acceptance."

If cemetery acceptance is critical → **confirm acceptance with the Cemetery Authority before drafting.**

The Professional Value of Saying No

Refusal is not failure — refusal preserves:

- statutory compliance,
- operational clarity,
- the cemetery's ability to act,
- and the notary's reputation and authority.

A notary who says yes improperly becomes part of the dispute.
A notary who says no properly prevents one.

Conclusion

Notaries must say **no** when:

- authority is unclear,
- consent is incomplete,
- spousal rights are unaddressed,
- the objective conflicts with the instrument,
- cemetery requirements are not met,
- or the signer seeks legal interpretation.

Clear boundaries ensure:

- enforceable instruments,
- reduced litigation

CHAPTER 14

WORKING WITH CEMETERIES, FUNERAL HOMES, AND COURTS

Cemetery-related notarial practice requires coordination with entities that each hold **distinct statutory or operational responsibilities**:

- **Cemeteries** control operational acceptance and interment logistics,
- **Courts** determine legal rights when authority is unresolved,
- **Funeral homes** manage the disposition of remains and interface with families.

The notary's role is to:

- **document authority** so these entities can act,
- **facilitate clarity**, not interpret law,
- and **avoid becoming a party to conflict** between stakeholders.

> + **CORE PRINCIPLE:**
> *The notary prepares instruments that allow others to act – the notary does not act in their place.*

Working with Cemeteries – Understanding Operational Primacy

Cemeteries have operational primacy over:

- acceptance of instruments,
- scheduling of interments,
- internal mapping and recordkeeping,
- installation approvals,
- and application of cemetery rules and regulations.

Even with proper notarial documentation, cemeteries may:

- refuse to act without additional signatures,
- require internal forms,
- require confirmation of spousal status,
- require proof of successor authority,
- or require **court orders** in certain disinterment cases.

Notarial boundary:

The notary cannot require a cemetery to accept an instrument.

Practical implication:
Before drafting, confirm:

- whether the cemetery requires a **specific form**,
- whether **spousal joinder** is mandatory,
- whether a **court order** is needed for disinterment regardless of consent,
- and whether **transfer forms** must be recorded in cemetery records.

COMMUNICATING WITH CEMETERIES – EXPECTATIONS

When contacting a cemetery:

- state **the instrument you are preparing**,
- verify **what they require**,
- avoid **interpreting their policies**,
- confirm **method of delivery** (email, mail, in-person),
- and request **confirmation of receipt.**

Recommended communication phrasing:

"I am preparing an instrument documenting authority regarding Space ___ at your cemetery. Please confirm your requirements for acceptance so the document may be drafted accordingly."

This avoids implying that your document **binds** the cemetery.

WORKING WITH COURTS – RECOGNIZING JURISDICTIONAL BOUNDARIES

Courts become involved when:

- authority is disputed,
- signatures are missing for disinterment,
- successors disagree about placement,
- title or lineage cannot be documented,
- or cemetery administration requires judicial confirmation.

Notarial boundary:

The notary does not file petitions, request orders, or interpret court outcomes.

Notaries may:

- authenticate signatures on **petitions prepared by counsel**,
- authenticate **consents** accompanying court filings,
- and prepare **affidavits of fact** used in proceedings,
  but must **not** characterize legal effect or likelihood of judicial outcome.

Required refusal phrasing when asked for litigation guidance:

"I cannot advise on court requirements. If consents are incomplete or disputed, judicial involvement may be necessary."

WHEN COURTS OVERRIDE DOCUMENTATION

Even if a notary prepares:

- a complete transfer,
- a valid acknowledgment,
- or unanimous disinterment consent,

a court may still:

- reject documentation based on procedural requirements,
- require **additional parties to be notified**,
- or issue orders affecting burial or disinterment despite agreements.

Implication:
Notarial documentation **facilitates action** – it does **not guarantee judicial acceptance**.

Working with Funeral Homes – Coordinating Without Advising

Funeral homes:

- transport remains,
- prepare death certificates,
- assist families with disposition decisions,
- act as intermediaries with cemeteries,
- and maintain regulatory compliance under separate law.

Funeral homes may **request notarized instruments** to:

- verify authority for burial,
- verify authority for cremation placement,
- document the successor agreement before scheduling.

Notarial boundary:

The notary confirms authority – the funeral home confirms disposition details.

Notaries must **not:**

- advise on funeral home pricing,
- confirm compliance with funeral regulations,
- certify the identity of remains,
- or interpret the cremation authorization law.

Chain of Communication – Recommended Sequence

A practical order of operations before drafting:

1. **Confirm family objective**
   (transfer, burial authorization, monument placement, etc.)
2. **Verify cemetery requirements**
   (form type, spousal clauses, delivery format)
3. **Identify required signatures**
   (spouse, successors, children, siblings, etc.)
4. **Determine the correct instrument**
   (transfer, relinquishment, acknowledgment, affidavit, authorization)
5. **Draft instrument** consistent with both
   Title 8 and **cemetery requirements**
6. **Authenticate execution**
7. **Deliver documents** to the cemetery with proof of delivery
8. **Confirm acceptance** where possible

Analytical rule:
Requirements before drafting → drafting before execution → delivery before reliance.

Avoiding Stakeholder Conflict

The notary must remain neutral when:

- siblings disagree on future burial,
- spouse refuses to sign a waiver,
- cemetery and family have differing expectations,
- funeral home seeks authorization faster than the family can agree.

Neutral phrasing:

"I prepare documents once authority and consent are clear.
I cannot move forward until the required parties agree or the court resolves the matter."

This avoids:

- taking sides,
- providing legal interpretation,
- or appearing to validate one party's claim.

When a Cemetery's Internal Rules Are Stricter Than Statutory Requirements

If a cemetery requires:

- **formal relinquishment** when statute would not,
- **spousal consent** for monument placement,
- **court order** for all disinterments,

the notary must comply with the **operational requirement** unless:

- the cemetery seeks to violate the law **and** requests the notary's involvement.

If cemetery policy exceeds statutory minimums:

Comply — operational authority governs acceptance.

If cemetery policy contradicts the statute:

Refer parties to counsel — notary does not mediate conflict of law.

Escalation Path When Stakeholders Disagree

When documentation cannot be accepted due to disagreement:

1. **Stop drafting**
2. **Explain the requirement for unanimous consent or court resolution**
3. **Avoid proposing a legal strategy**
4. **Provide a neutral statement of the next procedural step**

Neutral statement:

"Consent is incomplete. I cannot proceed. Unresolved authority may require legal counsel or court involvement."

Avoid:

- identifying which party should concede,
- interpreting the relative strength of positions,
- or recommending a litigation strategy.

Recognizing When Drafting Should Pause — Not End

Drafting should **pause** when:

- signatures are pending but expected,
- cemetery is reviewing requirements,
- death certificates are being issued,
- or successor contact is in progress.

Drafting should **end** when:

- authority will not be resolved,
- signatures are permanently refused,
- or disagreements escalate into legal conflict.

Pause for logistics — end for disputes.

Professional Reputation and Neutrality

Cemetery work is **community work**. Successors often return decades later to resolve authority — and will remember whether a notary:

- respected boundaries,
- remained neutral,
- or "took sides."

Reputation Principle:
The notary remembered for neutrality becomes the notary the families return to.

CONCLUSION

Working with cemeteries, courts, and funeral homes requires:

- **neutral communication,**
- **clear procedural boundaries,**
- **verification of requirements before drafting,**
- **delivery and proof of acceptance,**
- and **declination when authority is incomplete.**

Notarial practice succeeds when it **enables others to act** without:

- interpreting law,
- deciding disputes,
- or guaranteeing acceptance.

Documentation is the notary's contribution — execution and enforcement belong to others.

CONCLUSION

This concluding chapter distills the principles developed throughout the book into **practical, repeatable guidance** for notaries who work with cemetery-related instruments in Louisiana. The goal is not to summarize, but to **solidify a practice mindset** rooted in clarity, neutrality, and statutory awareness.

> ✚ **CORE PRINCIPLE:**
> *A cemetery notary ensures continuity of authority – not by interpreting law, but by documenting agreement clearly enough that the cemetery, the family, and the future can rely on it.*

THE NOTARY'S FUNCTION IN CEMETERY MATTERS

In ordinary transactions, notarial work may conclude once an instrument is executed. In cemetery matters, executed instruments may be relied upon for **generations**, at moments of loss, conflict, grief, or transition.

Therefore:

- **precision is not optional,**
- **neutrality is not negotiable, and**
- **retention is not clerical – it is stewardship.**

The Louisiana cemetery system relies on documents that prevent disputes—or resolve them without litigation—long after the original signatories are gone.

THE THREE FILTERS OF CEMETERY NOTARIAL PRACTICE

Across the entire book, three analytical filters recur. They form the **decision framework** that keeps cemetery documentation reliable:

FILTER 1 – OBJECTIVE

What are the parties trying to accomplish?

Clarify early:

- transfer?
- waiver of rights?
- authorization?
- consolidation?
- acknowledgment?
- or documentation of lineage?

Unclear objective → pause before drafting.

FILTER 2 – AUTHORITY

Who holds the power to authorize the intended action?

Confirm:

- recorded owners,
- successors,
- spouse status,

- statutory priorities under **La. R.S. 8:655**,
- and cemetery requirements.

Authority unclear → decline to draft.

FILTER 3 – CONSENT

Are the required signatories present — and willing?

Confirm unanimity when required:

- Always for the interment of a non-owner
- Sometimes for **disinterment**,
- often for **waivers**,
- cemetery-dependent for **monument installation**,
- never assumed away for **spousal rights**.

Consent incomplete → refer to counsel or court if parties insist on action.

NEUTRALITY AS A PROFESSIONAL DISCIPLINE

Neutrality is not passive – it is an **active restraint**:

- document, do not interpret;
- authenticate, do not advise;
- confirm, do not decide;
- clarify, do not persuade.

Neutrality signals:

- that the notary is **not a stakeholder**,

- that **no party has been favored,**
- and that **documentation rests on uncontested authority**.

Neutrality maxim:
The more contested the issue, the more restrained the notary must be.

WHY SAYING "NO" IS A PROFESSIONAL SKILL

A cemetery notary who cannot decline requests responsibly will:

- overstep authority,
- produce unusable instruments,
- or become entangled in family disputes.

A cemetery notary who **can** say no:

- protects the chain of authority,
- prevents future litigation,
- and maintains long-term credibility.

Conclusion:
Refusal is not rejection — it is protection of the public and the future.

The Role of Cemeteries, Funeral Homes, and Courts – And the Notary's Place Among Them

- **Cemeteries** determine operational acceptance.
- **Funeral homes** manage the disposition of remains.
- **Courts** resolve disputes and gaps in authority.
- **Notaries** document agreements and identity so others may act.

A notary who understands this allocation of roles avoids:

- giving legal opinions to families,
- interpreting statutes for cemeteries,
- or appearing to override cemetery policy.

Balanced Principle:
The notary opens doors – the cemetery decides whether to let someone through; the court settles who holds the key.

Successor and Spousal Rights – The Heart of Continuity

Two realities shape cemetery practice more than any others:

1. **successor rights do not disappear through silence**, and
2. **spousal burial rights persist until relinquished.**

Every reliable cemetery instrument:

- acknowledges lineage,
- addresses spousal rights,
- and maintains clarity for future generations.

Continuity commandment:
If spousal rights are ignored, the future will reopen the matter.

RECORDKEEPING – LEGACY BEYOND THE WORKPLACE

A cemetery notary's work outlives the notary.

Records:

- preserve authority across transitions,
- allow cemeteries to act decades later,
- prevent successors from needing court intervention,
- and provide families with certainty at vulnerable moments.

Recordkeeping ethos:
Every preserved document is a gift to a future successor who will need it more than the present signer ever imagined.

Operational Acceptance – The Quiet Power of Cemeteries

The law grants rights; cemeteries determine **how those rights are operationalized** within their grounds.

Therefore:

- **validity does not equal acceptance**,
- **acceptance does not equal adjudication**,
- and **documentation must meet both statutory and operational requirements**.

The notary acknowledges this reality without:

- pressuring cemetery staff,
- interpreting policy,
- or prescribing legal outcomes.

Operational maxim:
Document clearly – submit respectfully – defer to acceptance.

Future Challenges and Continuing Practice

Cemetery practice evolves through:

- demographic changes,
- increasing cremation,
- mobility of families,
- and administrative turnover.

These shifts create **greater reliance on written instruments** because oral tradition does not travel across distance or generations.

The notary becomes the link between:

- yesterday's recorded owner,
- today's successors,
- and tomorrow's unknown user of the space.

Final Guidance — Principles for Practice

These principles synthesize the entire book:

1. **Clarity precedes drafting.**
2. **Authority must be documented, not assumed.**
3. **Spousal rights persist unless relinquished.**
4. **Unanimous consent governs disinterment.**
5. **Disposition authority is not the same as interment authority.**
6. **A notary documents agreement — a court resolves disagreement.**
7. **Cemeteries control operational acceptance.**
8. **Recordkeeping ensures future reliance.**
9. **Neutrality protects the notary — and the family.**
10. **Declination is often the correct professional response.**

Final maxim:
A cemetery notary does not resolve the past — they preserve authority so the future is less burdened by it.

Closing Reflection

Cemetery notarial practice is work at the intersection of **law, memory, family, and permanence**.

Every instrument — drafted well or drafted poorly — shapes how future generations understand where they belong and who they follow.

By maintaining:

- restraint,
- precision,
- neutrality,
- and preservation,

The notary helps ensure that the dignity of the dead, the wishes of the living, and the order of the law remain aligned.

That is the essence of **cemetery stewardship** in notarial practice.

APPENDIX A

SAMPLE CEMETERY CLAUSES FOR NOTARIAL USE IN LOUISIANA

These clauses are intended as **sample language components** that a Louisiana Notary Public may use when preparing or receiving instruments relating to cemetery property, rights of interment, and ancillary cemetery matters.

Clauses are **modular** and may be incorporated into acts of sale, donation, exchange, transfer, stipulation, quitclaim, authorization, or affidavit as appropriate to the circumstances.

Notaries must ensure that the final instrument **accurately reflects the intent of the parties** and complies with **Louisiana law, including Title 8** of the Louisiana Revised Statutes. Complete Forms are available in *The Louisiana Cemetery Forms Book.*

CLAUSES REGARDING OWNERSHIP OF CEMETERY SPACES

OWNERSHIP AS IMMOVABLE PROPERTY UNDER SEPARATE TITLE

"The Parties acknowledge and agree that the cemetery space(s) described herein constitute **immovable property held in separate title**, consistent with Louisiana Revised Statutes Title 8, and that transfer of same conveys **only the right of interment**, subject to the rules and regulations of the Cemetery Authority."

Transfer of Record Ownership Without Warranty

"Appearer(s) hereby transfer, assign, and convey to the Transferee **all right, title, and interest** held of record to rights of interment in the cemetery space(s) described below, **without warranty of title**, and subject to all recorded restrictions, cemetery rules, and applicable law."

Clauses Regarding Right of Interment

Assignment of Right of Interment

"Appearer(s) hereby assign the **right of interment** in the cemetery space(s) described below to the designated Beneficiary(ies), reserving no rights thereto, and recognizing such rights as **personal rights** that do not constitute ownership of real property."

Revocation or Withdrawal of Interment Consent

To be used when having executed a Notarial Declaration granting someone a future right of interment in a space, without having transferred ownership

"Appearer(s) hereby **revoke and withdraw any previously granted interment consent**, reserving no current right except as stated herein, without prejudice to any interment already performed or authorized under Title 8."

Clauses Regarding Spousal Consent / La. R.S. 8:805

Spousal Consent to Interment

"Pursuant to La. R.S. **8:805**, the undersigned spouse hereby **consents to the interment** of the person designated below in the cemetery space(s) described herein, recognizing such consent as binding unless revoked in writing before interment."

Spousal Renunciation of Right of Interment

"The undersigned spouse hereby **renounces any statutory right of interment** granted pursuant to La. R.S. 8:805, reserving no priority or claim inconsistent with this act."

Spousal Confirmation of Prior Interment Authorization

"The undersigned spouse hereby **confirms and ratifies** all prior written authorizations for interment executed in favor of the deceased, with full recognition of La. R.S. 8:805."

Affidavit Clauses for Heirship & Authority

Affidavit of Heirship for Cemetery Purposes

"Affiant appears and states under oath that the deceased person named below died intestate, and that the following individuals are, **to the best of Affiant's knowledge**, the heirs who hold **priority or authority** regarding interment or disinterment consistent with Title 8 and applicable succession law."

Affidavit Establishing Interment Priority

"Affiant declares under oath that **no person with higher legal priority** to authorize interment exists or is reasonably known, and that Affiant is authorized to act under Title 8 and the rules of the Cemetery Authority."

Affidavit of No Objection to Interment

"Affiant affirms under oath that Affiant has **no objection to the interment** of the deceased person specified below in the cemetery space(s) described, and knows of **no living person** with a superior claim or objection."

Disinterment Clauses

Notaries should remind appearers that disinterment requires Cemetery Authority approval and may require additional authorizations under Title 8.

Consent to Disinterment

"Appearer(s) hereby grant **consent to disinterment** of the remains of the deceased person listed below, subject to approval by the Cemetery Authority and compliance with **La. R.S. 8:659** or other applicable law."

Limited Consent to Disinterment for Cremation or Relocation

"Appearer(s) hereby consent to **disinterment solely for the purpose of cremation or relocation**, reserving no further rights except as otherwise provided by law."

Objection to Disinterment

"Appearer(s) hereby **object to disinterment** of the deceased person named below and request that the Cemetery Authority deny any application inconsistent with this objection."

Clauses for Commingled or Communal Interment (Including Ossuary/Columbarium)

Consent to Commingled Interment

"Appearer(s) hereby grant **consent to commingled or communal placement** of cremated human remains within a designated ossuary or communal chamber, with recognition that **separate retrieval or division** is not possible."

Authorization for Placement of Cremated Remains

"Appearer(s) authorize the **placement of cremated remains** of the deceased person named below into the specified columbarium niche or ossuary, with acknowledgment of cemetery regulations and the **irrevocable nature** of the interment."

Clauses for Transfer on Death / Conditional Directions

*Note: Louisiana does **not** provide a statutory "transfer on death" deed concept for cemetery spaces – these clauses are **directional statements**, not dispositive instruments.*

Direction for Interment Upon Death (Nonbinding Personal Declaration)

"Appearer declares a **personal wish** to be interred in the cemetery space(s) described, recognizing that **final authority** shall be determined in accordance with Title 8 and applicable succession law."

DESIGNATION OF PREFERRED RIGHT OF INTERMENT (SUBJECT TO LAW)

"Appearer expresses a **preference** that the individual(s) named below exercise priority for interment decisions, recognizing that such preference is **subordinate to statutory authority**."

Complete Forms with statutory language can be found in *The Louisiana Cemetery Forms Book*

GLOSSARY OF KEY TERMS

Cemetery law uses terms that resemble those of property law but operate differently due to **spousal burial rights, succession rules, and public health considerations**.

This glossary defines **key terms** used in Title 8, related statutes, and notarial practice to ensure clarity of meaning when reading statutes, communicating with cemeteries, or interpreting documentation.

TERMS – DEFINED FOR CEMETERY CONTEXT

Abandonment (of cemetery or space)
Failure to maintain interment space or cemetery such that the public authority or Cemetery Authority may act under statutory processes. Does **not automatically extinguish interment rights**.

Acknowledgment (notarial)
A notarial act that confirms a signer personally appeared, was identified, and executed a document. **Does not transfer rights.**

Administrative acceptance (cemetery)
Recognition by the cemetery that presented documentation is **sufficient to proceed operationally**, not a certification of legal effect.

Affidavit of heirship
A written statement of facts documenting successors to the right of interment **without adjudicating disputes**. Used to support later instruments.

Assignment (cemetery context)
Designation of **a person to be buried in a space in which burial rights are owned without divesting oneself of ownership of rights.**

Authorization for disinterment
Written consent by **all persons required under La. R.S. 8:659** permitting removal of remains. Does not have to be unanimous unless there are only two heirs.

Authority to act
Ability to authorize interment, disinterment, or placement. May arise from **succession, spouse status, assignment, or relinquishment.**

Burial record(s)
Documentation maintained by a cemetery that shows the location, date, and identity of interments. Separate from **purchase contracts** or **ownership records.**

Chain of authority
The sequence of instruments and facts that demonstrate **who may act at any point in time** regarding a cemetery space.

Cemetery Authority
An entity or person exercising operational oversight of a cemetery under Title 8.

Cemetery space
A location designated for interment or placement of remains. **Right of interment is not identical to ownership of land.**

Communal interment / Ossuary
Placement of cremated remains in a communal structure or chamber. May limit future retrieval **depending on program policy**, not altered by notarization.

Consent (disinterment)
Written authorization by all persons required under law. **Consent is mandatory unless judicial authorization is granted.**

Court authorization
Judicial order permitting disinterment or resolving disputes over authority. **Supersedes conflicting private documentation.**

Delivery record
Evidence that documents were provided to the cemetery or stakeholders, supporting **future reliance** and **operational clarity**.

Disposition of remains
Placement of human remains by burial, entombment, or cremation. **Authority follows La. R.S. 8:655.**

Disinterment
Removal of remains from an interment location. Requires **majority consent** or **court order**.

Family successor
An heir who succeeds to the right of interment through lineage, **documented but not adjudicated**, via affidavit or other instruments.

Interment
Placement of human remains in a grave, crypt, or niche.

Majority consent (La. R.S. 8:655)
For disposition of remains, the **majority of adult children** may act when no spouse survives, and no priority claimant exists.

Memorialization
Installation of a marker or monument. May require **separate authority documentation** from the interment authority.

Mutual waiver of burial rights
An instrument in which co-owners relinquish their **rights to one person**, consolidating authority.

Notarial refusal
Decision not to draft an instrument when it would bypass statutory consent, misstate authority, or require legal interpretation.

Operational acceptance
Cemetery confirmation that documentation is **sufficient to proceed** with burial, installation, or record update.

Purchase agreement (contract)
Agreement for cemetery space. Establishes **initial recorded owner** but does not displace statutory spousal rights.

Record of interment
Entry documenting burial or placement in cemetery records. Does **not** determine the current authority.

Relinquishment (individual)
Voluntary surrender of right of interment. Often necessary to resolve **in-indivision** interests.

Right of interment
Right to be interred in, or authorize interment within, a designated space. **Distinct from ownership or control of land.**

Signatory authority
Ability to validly sign documentation affecting cemetery actions. Determined by **Title 8 and successor status**, not by convenience.

Spousal burial rights (La. R.S. 8:805)
Vested right of a surviving spouse to be interred with or among marital family burial spaces, **unless waived**.

Successor authority
Authority possessed by heirs to act regarding cemetery spaces **once documented**, typically through affidavit or succession.

Transfer
An instrument that **divests** the right of interment from one owner to another. Requires addressing **spousal rights**.

General Index

A

Acknowledgment
legal effect vs. authentic acts 11–13, 57–60
limitations in transfers 89–91, 96–98
drafting insufficiencies 100–104, 109–114
successor authority verification 117–123

Affidavit of heirship
evidentiary role in proving successor authority 49–52, 92–98
limitations without authentic act 100–104, 107–114
cemetery acceptance vs. legal sufficiency 117–123

Assignment (authority to control interment)
distinction from interment-right transfer 26–30, 65–70
successor conflicts 71–77
acceptance defects and failures 79–82

Authentic acts
required form for transfer of interment rights 11–16, 27–31
community-property considerations 55–57, 59–63
identification of successor authority 64–68, 119–123

C

Cemetery acceptance
operational discretion 2, 4–6, 41–42, 74, 144–145
declining documents 147–153, 161–164, 173–176

Conveyances of cemetery rights
transfer by authentic act....13, 27–29, 37
identification of successor authority....61–62

D

Disinterment
requirements for authority documentation.... 11–16, 22–27
majority vs. unanimity misunderstandings.... 37–41, 43–45
cemetery refusal and court intervention 46–52, 61–72
successor conflicts....79–82
drafting considerations....118–120, 136–138, 148–150

Drafting limitations
neutrality and refusal to notarize.... 5–8, 13–15, 25, 30
avoiding practice of law 41–42, 47–50
authority verification before drafting.... 56–58, 65, 71–73
protecting against insufficient documentation 99–101, 112–114
withdrawal when improper...117–123, 137–144, 159–160, 164–165

F

Forms
integration with successor authority 11–13, 19, 23, 28–29
supporting transfer instruments.... 36–37, 40–41
major form sets in authority verification 54–58, 92–104
correction and supplemental documentation.... 107–114, 119–123

H

Heirship
successor determination and documentation 1, 5–7, 12–16, 25
interaction with interment rights 27–29, 36–38, 40, 49, 51–52
limitations for transfer instruments 55–57, 59–63
authority chain clarity 80–84, 94–100
recurrent evidentiary defects 102–106, 109–111

I

Identification of cemetery space
precision required for transfer documents 23–26, 33–37
alignment with successor authority.................... 52–53, 56–57, 59–60
major drafting failures.............94–100, 102–106, 109–111, 121–125

Interment rights
nature distinct from land ownership 11–13, 27–33
successor authority and transfer 42–45, 49–52, 55–57, 59–63
authority confirmation requirements 68–69, 73–75, 77
recordation expectations... 79–84, 94–100
limitations of use 102–106, 109–111, 114–116

M

Mutual waiver agreements
consolidating successor authority 12, 14, 26, 29, 36–37
requirements and limitations............................. 49–52, 55–57, 59–63
successor conflicts and drafting applications 68–69, 73–75
withdrawal when insufficient 94–100, 109–111, 114–116
cemetery acceptance 160–161, 178

N

Notarial declarations
assignment of authority to direct interment..........................3, 25, 29
marital status and successor clauses........................... 46, 72–73, 136

S

Spousal burial rights
priority and successor-status protections.... 3–5, 8, 15–19, 25–26, 30
major transfer considerations.................................. 33–36, 38–42, 45
community-property implications.................... 49–52, 55–57, 59–63
interaction with authentic acts................................ 68–69, 73–75, 77
inferior documentation and corrections 94–100, 109–111, 114–116

Succession documentation
authority confirmation...25, 40, 42
relationship to transfer instruments 51–52, 55–57, 59–63
major defects in verification 68–69, 73–75, 77
correction....................... 94–100, 109–111, 114–116, 119–125, 127
cemetery acceptance... 150–151, 163–164

W

Waiver of burial rights
release of successor authority........................... 12, 16, 24, 35, 38, 40
requirements and limitations............................ 50–52, 55–57, 59–63
major drafting considerations................................. 73–75, 77, 80–84
correction & supplementation94–100, 102–106, 109–111, 114–116
acceptance.... 130–133, 136, 138–139, 154–155, 163, 166, 176, 178

WEB RESOURCES

The following online resources provide direct access to Louisiana cemetery law, regulatory agencies, and related guidance. These sites were referenced or relied upon in preparing this handbook:

- **The Louisiana Cemetery Handbook & Louisiana Cemetery Forms Books**
  Official website for this Handbook and the Forms Book
  https://LaCemeteryBook.com

- **Louisiana Revised Statutes, Title 8 (Cemeteries)**
  Official compilation of Louisiana cemetery laws.
  https://www.legis.la.gov/legis/Laws_Toc.aspx?folder=82&title=8

- **Louisiana Cemetery Board**
  The regulatory body overseeing cemeteries in Louisiana provides rules, compliance materials, and forms.
  https://lcb.la.gov

- **Louisiana Legislature – Laws and Codes**
  Access to all Louisiana statutes, including Title 8.
  https://www.legis.la.gov/legis/LawSearch.aspx

- **Louisiana Department of Health – Vital Records**
  Guidance on death certificates and authorizations that may intersect with burial and disinterment procedures.
  https://ldh.la.gov/vitalrecords

- **Louisiana Attorney General Opinions**
  Opinions interpreting cemetery law and related issues.
  https://www.ag.state.la.us/Opinions

NOTES

NOTES

NOTES

NOTES

NOTES

NOTES

NOTES

Made in United States
Orlando, FL
04 November 2026

90200303R00115